Beyond the Classroom Walls

Beyond the Classroom Walls
ETHNOGRAPHIC INQUIRY AS PEDAGOGY

June A. Gordon

RoutledgeFalmer
Taylor & Francis Group

NEW YORK AND LONDON

Portions of chapter 1 appeared in earlier versions in "Asian American Resistance to Selecting Teaching as a Career: The Power of Community and Tradition," *Teachers College Record,* 102(1): 173–196, 2000. Reprinted by permission of Blackwell Publishing, Ltd.

An earlier version of chapter 4 appeared in *Teaching Education,* 8(1): 55–64, 1996. Reprinted by permission of the University of South Carolina.

An earlier version of chapter 7 appeared as "It's a Fine Line. Deconstructing Youth at Risk: Critical Ethnography as Pedagogy," in *Action in Teacher Education,* 22(2): 13–24, 2000.

RoutledgeFalmer
29 West 35th Street
New York, NY 10001
www.routledge-ny.com

Published in Great Britain by
RoutledgeFalmer
11 New Fetter Lane
London EC4P 4EE
www.routledgefalmer.com

Copyright © 2002 by Taylor & Francis Books, Inc.

RoutledgeFalmer is an imprint of the Taylor & Francis Group.
Printed in the United States of America on acid-free paper.

10 9 8 7 6 5 4 3 2 1

Library of Congress Cataloging–in–Publication Data
is available from the Library of Congress.

Beyond the Classroom Walls: Ethnographic Inquiry as Pedagogy -
June A. Gordon

ISBN 0-415-93494-x (pbk.) 0-415-93493-1

To my husband,
with love.

Contents

Acknowledgments

THE TEACHING EXPERIENCES SHARED IN THIS WORK HAVE GREATLY depended upon the collaboration and trust established with students and teachers in the state of Washington, in particular, Seattle, Bellingham, Oak Harbor, and Tacoma, and in California, most notably in San Jose, San Francisco, and Santa Cruz.

While I have been influenced by many individuals, I am most indebted to those who felt that my approach to preparing people to work in difficult ubran settings was worth sharing with a much wider audience. Two individuals, Professors Patricia Stoddart and Barbara Gottesman, encouraged me over a period of four years to move to publish these case studies. Bill Moore of the Washington State Board for Community Colleges played an essential role in sponsoring my research in several community colleges in Washington State. I would like to thank district administrators, Rudy Herrera and Charles Parchment, who not only supported my research on teacher attitudes toward low-income students but also welcomed me and 200 of my students over a three-year period of time into their schools in California. We hope we contributed as much as we received. And finally, my thanks to Joe Miranda of RoutledgeFalmer who was pivotal in getting the manuscript to press in an expeditious manner.

Introduction

TRANSFORMATIVE PEDAGOGY RECOGNIZES THE SEARCH FOR MEANING AND its place in schooling. The effort to create meaning—to find one's place or identity—faces everyone. It is a constructive process in dialogue with self and other, however variant or deviant the expression might be (Bruner, 1990; Rosaldo, 1993). The child uses immediate, specific materials to create a local identity: family, home, school; the teenager requires something less local, perhaps even national or universal in scope—the so-called youthful idealism. Pedagogy on a local level transmits the cultural basics that children need to enter the negotiation for the mature identities they will seek (Spindler et al., 1990). For high school and college students, pedagogy that remains local loses its relevance for larger meanings. Normally we expect the family, church, or other institutions—scouts, sports, fraternities, YM/WCAs—to develop these larger meanings or values. When these fail us, we face career choices in a vacuum. The academic instruments of the school—grades, tests, and limited personal guidance—fail to address youthful confusion, which requires value-based commitment to prepare for a career; otherwise, the process of job hunting remains an uninspired search for economic security and a life without meaningful work.

Critical dialogue with self and others through ethnographic research provides a transformative pedagogy. It assumes that relationships within institutions can be revived, enlivened, and improved when impediments to student success are identified. This requires the involvement of all concerned. The needs and goals of each group shape the values of pedagogy. In trying to capture the whole process, my approach shows the impact of ethnographic methods on those studied as well as those who do the studying. The research process reveals the nature of the educational situation under view and offers professional educators a path to understanding their students as well as their own workplace. The goal of my work as an educator is dialogue conducted and discovered within a critical interpretation of the circumstances in which we live. While my work has been largely one of self-discovery, I recognize the many sources in the work of critical and feminist pedagogy (Greene, 1986; Deever, 1990; McLaren, 1989), constructivist psychology, Foucault's "care of the self" (1988), Friere's dialogic pedagogy (1970), Bruner's meaning-making and narrative truth (1990), the work of Ogbu (1995, 1998) and Geertz (1973) on ethnographic, local research in community meanings of schooling, critical race theory (Stanfield, 1994), and the several strands of critical ethnography (Carspecken, 1996).

Ethnographic research combines intensive, local inquiry through interviews and observation with attention to contextual factors that structure local events. By enabling them to reflect on their reasoning, ethnographic research can have the transformative outcome of empowering those interviewed. Rist (1994) refers to this as the "enlightenment function" in contrast to the "engineering function." With enlightenment comes recognition of one's condition and the possibility of acting upon this knowledge (Mishler, 1986). While some may question the action role of research, Macedo, in a discussion with Freire (Freire & Macedo, 1995), argues that "dialogue as a process of learning and knowing must always involve a political project with the objective of dismantling oppressive structures and mechanisms prevalent both in education and society" (p. 380).

Transformative research embraces engagement and accepts subjectivity. Interviewer and interviewee move together in a reflective and reflexive dance. McDermott (1976) speaks of this process as people in interaction becoming environments for each other. While power indisputably remains in the hands of the researcher, the researcher is also at the mercy of the informant (Fairclough, 1989). Authentic information flows after the establishment of trust. Demonstrating one's worth often comes at the risk of self-disclosure, something seldom welcomed in traditional academic research circles. Oakley (1981) recognizes the risk of personal involvement as "the condition under which people come to know each other and admit others into their lives" (p. 58). This is the essence of successful transformative ethnography.

I use a variety of pedagogical tools to conduct critical dialogues through ethnographic inquiry. These include self-portraiture, reflective writing, small group collaboration, field experience, interviews, presentations, and, in some contexts, even mandatory car pooling to research sites. I model an approach to teaching for educators and reveal to them the needs of students of color, immigrants, and first-generation college students within higher education. As the students in search of their own understanding reach into schools, homes, and agencies, they in turn activate the understanding of those they reach. Their realization of that effect in turn enhances their commitment to the teaching and research process, moving them into classrooms as researchers as well as teachers. The overall process demonstrates the conclusion of many others that undergraduate involvement in teaching, research, and service is the best form of retention. In the face of high attrition rates for Mexican American and African American students, Claude Steele (1992) has suggested that such involvement is essential. My goal is to enhance student success through a cohort of diverse students working in collaboration with each other and their instructors as well as with all segments of the community. They learn through research, which in turn can bear on the needs of the community

Since the 1990s, in an effort to comprehend the impediments that students of color and working-class students face in accessing education, I have used ethnography as a research tool in many different contexts: universities, four-year colleges, community colleges, K–12 schools, and several alternative education programs. The individuals interviewed have spanned a variety of perspectives, including those of administrators, teachers, students, community workers, and parents. The research itself can be a tool of critical intervention, which not only allows individuals to reflect on their decisions and opinions but also allows for contradiction and transformation. As a teacher educator, I have wanted to share the power and joy that comes at such pivotal moments in the life of my students when they move from one point of awareness and cognition to another. Consequently, all my students have participated in ethnographic research, which provids for a "reality check" for those who have very little knowledge of the population that they intend to serve as educators.

The foundations for my own research will enable the reader to understand the pedagogy I have developed. Although I grew up in a multicultural, low-income urban community in California, my family background is working-class British. Reared by immigrant parents who were from two different ethnic and religious groups, I became an astute observer of differences. My childhood provided me with numerous opportunities to position myself as outsider as I negotiated with my African American, Asian, and Latino playmates the status markers of the day. I arrived at Stanford University at age seventeen; my parents had divorced—one living in the United States and the other in Australia—and my only sibling, a brother, had recently died. Never had I been around such wealth and such Whiteness. As a first-generation college student, I struggled to find the relevance of academia to my life. My return home (as a college drop-out) to England to work only heightened my awareness of my pariah status; I was no longer comfortable with the attitudes of my British working-class family.

Resuming my studies at Stanford and after living and teaching in Taiwan and Japan, I concentrated on East Asian Studies. With a facility in Japanese, Mandarin, and Spanish, I worked as a source language coordinator for computerized instruction in these and other languages and then as program director for international students at Stanford following my B.A. These cross-cultural experiences increased my interest and curiosity in how people construct meaning in their lives in ways that make sense to them. Several years later as a college administrator in Washington State, I formalized my qualitative orientation to life when I engaged in a research project that studied why the academic and personal needs of students of color on predominantly White college campuses were not being met. This research resulted in a master's degree in higher education and an invitation from John I. Goodlad to work with him at the Center for Educational Renewal (CER) of the University of Washington and pursue my Ph.D. in educational policy and leadership studies. My work in qualitative research springs from these numerous experiences as an outsider fascinated with the question of why people act and think the way they do.

The first major ethnographic study I designed was an attempt to understand the complexity of programs affecting minority students in six public four-year universities in the state of Washington. This research provided an interpretive analysis from the perspective of sixty administrators and faculty and staff members of the ways in which their campuses attempted to recruit and accommodate students of color. I used the insights of the informants to construct a critique of institutional strategies and attitudes toward polices designed to support or reinforce the cultural heritage of specific ethnic minority groups (Gordon, 1997a). My research on the value of minority culture-based programs set the stage for further exploration into:

1. ways for minority students to overcome the impediments they face in gaining educational access;
2. how administrators and teachers can work to help these students develop a strong identity;
3. how to recruit future teachers who are willing and able to teach students who are at risk of being marginalized within academia; and
4. how to develop the preparation and commitment needed to bring students into the teaching force sought for urban schools.

Realizing that the difficulties faced by first-generation college students, including many students of color, strongly related to their K–12 experience, I went on to develop a national research project focusing on the perspectives of teachers of color. In order to get a range of responses to the question "Why do so few students of color enter the field of teaching?" I interviewed over 160 teachers from the four standard categories: Native American, Latino, African American, and Asian American, in three large urban school districts in the United States: Cincinnati, Seattle, and Long Beach, California (Gordon, 1994, 1997b, 2000a). During this period of research I gained a variety of insights not only on the topic under discussion, that is, the shortage of minority teachers, but also on the multitude of ways kids who "fall through the cracks" are schooled. This led to research in several community colleges and alternative educational programs. For me, the quest to understand how working-class students and students of color negotiated the system required that I look at the range of institutions that offered support to these individuals. If I had stayed at the level of four-year universities, I could not have understood the complexity of issues nor unearthed the truths behind the mythologies of who is "at risk," who drops out, and who attends either community colleges or alternative programs, and for what reason.

I began my research in community colleges informally as an instructor for an urban campus of a four-year university. This led to an invitation to be a part of a national research team funded by a noteworthy foundation that was working to identify the characteristics of community colleges that have high transfer rates. One thing that dominated the findings was the high dropout rate of first-quarter community college students. My experience with urban community colleges led to an invitation from the Washington State Board of Community Colleges to train the staff and faculty of eight of their institutions in basic ethnographic fieldwork methodology in order for the state to begin to determine the causes of "early leavers" and provide some interventionist strategies. This experience served as a transition point from conducting my own research to training others in critical ethnography (Thomas, 1993). As I watched how the process transformed the lives of those I trained, as well as those of their informants, I saw the importance of creating similar experiences for my university students.

What I came to realize from this experience is that if I wanted to enhance the educational options of working-class students and students of color as well as provide safe spaces for educators to learn about these groups, I had to incorporate into my pedagogy opportunities for future teachers to have face to face experiences with youth and their communities. I also felt it imperative that I continue my own research on alternative educational programs as I sent my university students out into the community to explore a range of educational institutions and situations. This symbiotic relationship between teacher and student in which we were all in the process of learning forged a bond and level of trust and authenticity that created fertile ground for yet more revealing research and stronger pedagogy. Some of these alternative education programs included my work at an Indian heritage school for native children, an expulsion program for African American children, an urban academy, an alternative high school program called Middle College, and a drug and alcohol rehab program for upper middle-class White youth. All of these programs were radically different in their orientation, pedagogy, population, and rates of success. All provided insights into my overall quest to understand the reasons youth move out or drop out of the traditional educational system.

Lack of knowledge of the larger context of our students' lives as well as minimal and superficial communication between teachers and students from low-income communities have been two of the major stumbling blocks for effective teaching and learning and, hence, the retention of both marginalized students and middle-class teachers (Cummins, 1986; Villegas, 1988; Erikson, 1987). I contend that if future teachers do not connect with students and their families on a personal level prior to becoming professionals and commit to the education of these youth, they never will. Graduate school internships or student teaching is not the time to introduce future teachers to their clients. It is too late when the focus is on personal performance and not on the lives of the individuals whom they are to serve. Student teachers are in the process of being assessed as professionals. There is little time or inclination to get to know the students themselves, to find out who they are, why they are where they are, and what makes them view the world as they do. What hooks a person into a profession that is as demanding as teaching is the experience that one can truly make a difference in someone's life. The movement from wanting success for one's own sake, to wanting success for the client or child's sake is a moment of radical transformation. But the transition is essential if we are to not only attract the right people into the profession but if they are to stay and become effective educators.

PREVIEW OF THE BOOK

The purpose of this book is to provide examples of a pedagogy based on ethnographic research that:

1. engages all students in critical, complex learning;
2. assists in retaining students who perceive their lives as marginal to the academic endeavor;
3. engages students with their own communities; and
4. updates and renews educators' knowledge of students' lives, schools, and communities.

The first three chapters include examples of transformative pedagogy with undergraduate students, many of whom are considering teaching as a potential career. All of the situations described in these chapters come from teaching situations in California. Chapter 1, "Students Reengaging Their Home Communities," gives three examples of how student research groups, each completely different in its focus, returned to their respective communities to inquire about critical issues held of utmost importance to the students but left without validation within the university context. The process led to radical changes in attitude toward school, self-image, and future aspirations. Chapter 2, "Immigrants and Education: Dialogic Inquiry as Pedagogy," presents the story of undergraduate students, most of them first- or second-generation Americans, in a course that explores the adaptation process for a range of immigrant groups as they enter the American school system. The chapter reveals not only the similarities and differences in views and experiences among the groups and cultures represented in the interviews but also the growing awareness of the students' own stereotypes about immigration and schooling. Chapter 3, "Future Teachers Assist in Urban, Low-Income, Multicultural Classrooms," introduces the effort to place potential teachers as tutors and researchers in a highly diverse California school district that is attempting to respond to the economic and linguistic challenges of a large immigrant population. The experience served to provide assistance to teachers and students while simultaneously giving undergraduates an opportunity to interview teachers and students about their views on urban education. As a result, many altered their views about the concepts "urban" and "poverty" as well as about the significant role a caring adult can play in the life of children who need you, even if you only see them once a week.

Chapters 4, 5, and 6 offer accounts of work with graduate students who have made the commitment to teaching and are currently enrolled in credential programs. These chapters illustrate work done in three distinctly different teaching situations within Washington State. Chapter 4, "'Masks of Normality': Teacher Training on a Military Base," explores the assumptions many people hold about military personnel and members of their families becoming teachers. While teaching an evening class on a distant military base as part of the university's outreach credential program, I reflect on my own prejudices as the students' "masks of normality" fade during a course dedicated to looking at issues of inequality and injustice. Chapter 5, "Confronting the Larger Community of Helping Professionals," tells of one case study where this methodology was applied to increasing pre-service student awareness of, and engagement with, the larger community of helping professionals in the urban context that is home to their students. Visits to an array of social service agencies and interviews with individuals who work primarily with low-income youth and their families provide these future teachers with first-hand accounts of the larger context of their students' lives. Chapter 6, "Home Visits," presents three examples of an effort to use home visits as a means not only to make a better connection between home and school but also to expand both experienced and pre-service teachers' understanding of their students. Two of the narratives take place in a rural, predominantly Mexican, immigrant community; the other story reflects the transformation and education of a veteran teacher in an urban, predominantly African American part of a city.

Chapters 7 and 8 explain more fully the use of transformative pedagogy with veteran teachers and alternative educators who have returned to university for a master in education degree. In the first account the return seems a natural part of professional development, but in the second shifts in the economy and fate seem to cause the return. Chapter 7, "Deconstructing Youth At-Risk," is an account of how experienced teachers reexamined their assumptions and images of what constituted "at-riskness" and who actually faced risk of marginalization and alienation in their classrooms. This in turn led to a growing awareness that teachers themselves, and/or their families, often are, or have been, "at risk." Chapter 8, "Adult Educators Inquire into Workplace Stress," shares the research findings of a group of individuals who came together from very disparate and desperate lives ostensibly to acquire an advanced degree and tools to navigate in a mercurial economy but end up inquiring within their own workplace as to the causes of their displacement. Representing a host of educational settings, this chapter explains, often in the words of the students themselves, how they came to learn of, and cope with, stress, both personal and professional, as well as downsizing and unemployment in a major urban city.

Chapter 9, "First Quarter Attrition: Community College Staff and Faculty Ask Why," covers a statewide effort to train community college staff and faculty in ethnographic methodology in order not only to find out the reasons for the high number of first-quarter drop-outs but also to insure that the causes are attended to by those adults whose job it is to serve those students. Through both premeditated interviews and spontaneous conversations with students, faculty, and staff learn of the complexity of community college students' lives and the obstacles that they must confront daily. The "Afterword" briefly sets out a general outline of my approach and a few final thoughts.

CHAPTER 1

Students Reengaging Their Home Communities

ONE OF THE MOST SALIENT FORCES UNDERMINING HIGHER EDUCATION IS disengagement. Students leave college for a variety of reasons, but often it is due to an inability to find a connection between their personal lives prior to college and the work that is required for success in higher education. This is particularly true for students of color and working-class students who do not see the relevance of a detached liberal arts education to the demands of their lives "back home" (Duster, 1991; Astin, 1993). For many of these students, their past life was just that, passed, hidden, and disconnected from their current pursuits. This disjunction can cause resentment, friction, and distancing from the very environment they need to engage in order to succeed. For first-generation college students, the situation is compounded in a variety of ways.

First of all, there is the separation of self from family. While part of growing up involves creating a unique identity, when that development takes place in isolation from the family context the new identity can be perceived as determined by outside influences. The inability and the inappropriateness of sharing the realities of college life with one's family and friends can inhibit fluid communication and create distance. Intellectual growth at school can create emotional tension at home. For working-class students one might even ask if it is possible to really "go home" once you have been to university. Second, first-generation students experience separation of self from other

1

students. Isolation kicks in when working-class students on prestigious university campuses believe that they are alone in dealing with this schizophrenic existence. As a result, they resist sharing with peers, faculty, or staff members what is happening to them. They hesitate to talk about their past, their family, their trials, their lives "back home." Third, masking of self becomes a necessary survival skill. Political rhetoric and bravado at times are used to mask the confusion, loneliness, and academic gaps. Having to maintain a façade at both home and school drains energy that could be used for academic achievement. Fourth, as a result of separation, isolation, and masking, students do not reveal their need for assistance (Fullilove and Treisman, 1990). Working-class students may fear exposure of weaknesses, particularly if they have been accepted to an elite university and are the first to leave their community to attend college. Unaware of differences in cultural capital and how educational background favors some students over others, they would rather "go it alone" than collaborate with those whom they assume are different from them. They carry the burden of family pride mixed with fear of failure. In reality, they know that their success in the context of their community is moot in comparison to their middle- and upper-middle class college peers; revealing inadequacies would jeopardize their status. While they cannot go back, they fear moving forward as they lack the skills and knowledge to negotiate the system.

Knowing of this dilemma, as I have lived the experience myself, I reached out to my undergraduate students who perceived themselves as either "at risk" or marginalized. In collaboration, we designed intensive research projects that linked their prior lives to their current academic selves. The goal was to allow them to explore issues of identity and educational achievement within their own social, cultural, and ethnic communities. As noted in the work of Vasquez and others (1994) and Velez-Ibanez and Greenberg (1992), school knowledge can be empowering for subordinate groups, as long as it respects, and even draws upon, the cultural resources of those groups. Similarly, the retention data on first-generation college students, particularly if they are students of color, demonstrate that students who connect with a faculty member through research that is perceived as beneficial to both sides tend to achieve academically and graduate at a higher rate (Astin, 1993). Following the insights of Claude Steele (Hummel & Steele, 1996), I have found that engaging students in authentic research and inquiry brings about their own best efforts and eventual success. For these particular students, ethnographic research increased their retention and provided them with direction and confidence toward careers in public school teaching, counseling, and related professions. In short, I found that returning students to their communities as researchers provided a form of critical engagement that reached multiple goals.

The major goal of the work was to enhance student success through a cohort of diverse students working in collaboration with each other and with an instructor as well as with various individuals of their communities. It involved a process by which research bears on the needs of the community—a process that fosters the need to understand. The sources for this approach to the integration of research, teaching, and service are the many strands of critical pedagogy that seek to involve the student as an active participant in the learning process through cultural awareness and community service as developed by Freire (1970), Horton and Freire (1990), Shor (1980), Moses (see Chevidgney, 1996), and others. This approach also utilizes learning through research in schools and communities that enhance professional development in educators (Becker, 1998) as well as critical ethnography found in studies by Carspecken (1996) and others. Critical ethnographies that focus on students include Anyon (1995), Fine (1991), McLaren (1986), Connell, (1989), Weis (1985), MacLeod (1987), Holland and Eisenhart (1993), and Solomon (1992).

This chapter is not about the research findings from the undergraduate research projects but rather about the use of ethnographic research as pedagogy for engagement and retention. The three research groups that emerged from this effort focused on the absence of Asian Americans in the teaching force; Latina identity: colleges as settings for confusion; and gang affiliation and educational aspirations. In the following pages I will explain how these three groups were formed, how the research was conducted, and the nature of the transformative process for both informants and students. The groups consisted of students who had completed an undergraduate upper-division course with me that focused on theory and research related to the education of urban students. The course was titled "Minorities in the Schooling Process." In each case, students, unbeknownst to their peers, had either come to me personally or had written in one of their assignments about an issue or concern that was inhibiting their academic progress at the university. They all perceived that they were unique in their frustration or situation and were to some extent in "hiding." After I spoke with each of them at length and identified their concern, I inquired if they would be interested in meeting other students who were wrestling with the same or similar problems. For those that agreed, I offered the possibility of conducting research on their specific topic over an extended period of time. All were trained in basic qualitative research methods: how to identify respondents; how to open up dialogue around difficult issues; confidentiality; probes; and general ethnographic protocol. In some cases student researchers coded their own data; in most cases they transcribed and translated their own tapes or field notes.

ASIAN AMERICANS RESEARCH THE ABSENCE OF ASIAN AMERICANS IN THE TEACHING FORCE

The socially constructed population category "Asian" is a rather new phenomenon used by "outsiders" to denote individuals who live in or who have ancestry from a certain but rather large and widely varied geographical area. Seldom is this term used by Asians themselves. Rather they refer to themselves by their nationality: Chinese, Cambodian, Japanese, Filipino, and so on. Who defines what is Asia? Are Indians of the "subcontinent" Asian? Are Russians east of the Urals? Are Samoans? Ironically, Filipinos are often in a netherworld when it comes to their Asian identity, particularly in the United States. Since many Filipinos have Spanish surnames, they are often misidentified as Latino. Caught between the rejection by people of the East Asian communities as well as the Latino community, Filipinos, while one of the largest "minority" populations in California, are seldom acknowledged as a powerful force with which to contend.

During the last couple of weeks of the course, I watched with amazement as a group of Asian American students converted a presentation on the work of Lisa Delpit and other African American authors on Black English to a discussion of Asian, specifically Filipino, "Pidgin English." They based their resistance to the readings on the claim that the literature on diversity both in higher education and in K–12 schools minimized the voices of Asian Americans compared to African Americans and Latinos. For the first time all quarter, I heard the public voices of students who had refused to speak up or offer critique. Their presentation provided fascinating information that set the context for language variation in both historical and cultural context. Granted, the class had almost a hundred students in it but there were far more Asian Americans than there were African Americans enrolled and the latter had no problem stating their views. Having a background in East Asian studies myself, I understood the complexity of the socially constructed term "Asian" and how it masked tremendous diversity in terms of religion, language, ethnicity, and national identity. I was also aware of the divisions among supposedly intact groups based on time of immigration, time in country, and socioeconomic status. Yet, in this education class these students came together united around their apparent "oppression" and, at my invitation, came to talk to me individually about their concerns.

When asked how they proposed to alter not only the representation of Asians in the research literature but also the numbers of Asians in the teaching profession, they hesitated and acknowledged that they were unsure if they would ultimately choose teaching as their life's work even though they, as undergraduates, had already taken several courses in the education minor. In all cases the students believed that they were not in control of their occupational decisions, that there were larger forces at play coming from the community, their families, and their peers. They claimed that teaching was not an acceptable profession to their families and, as a result, they had been "in hiding" about their extensive coursework in education and any consideration of teaching as a career. Their feelings of frustration and impotence led me to invite them to explore how general these perceptions were among Asian American youth as well as to inquire with their families and community as to the source of their attitudes toward education and teaching as a profession. Although these meetings began informally, a pattern clearly emerged from each conversation, one that reinforced my previous research on Asian American attitudes toward perceived career options.

Having previously conducted research on the reasons students of color might be selecting teaching as a profession, I had some understanding of Asian American concerns as well as those of Latinos, African Americans, and Native Americans, at least within the three urban areas I had studied: Seattle, Cincinnati, and Long Beach, California. Out of these four major ethnic groups as represented by the 160 teachers of color I had interviewed, Asian Americans comprised only 20 of the informants due to their scarcity in the urban districts under study. The data from that research project indicated that Asian Americans resisted teaching as a career choice for three reasons: (1) personal feelings of inadequacy in dealing with the multiple social service demands placed on teachers in America, (2) the traditional image of teacher within Asian culture, and (3) the fear of teaching non-Asian children.

Of the thirteen Asian undergraduates in the class, nine agreed to participate in a group independent research project. They represented five different ethnic groups coming from a wide range of socioeconomic backgrounds: three Chinese, one Japanese, one Chinese born in Vietnam, one Vietnamese, two Filipinos, and one Korean; three males and six females. All were committed to the retention of their culture and had volunteered numerous times in their respective cultural and community organizations. Wanting to create a space for them to reflect more carefully on this process, I invited them to write about the circumstances that had brought them to the point where they were taking undergraduate education courses that were intended to prepare teachers for urban schools. Given that this curricular decision could potentially be in conflict with parental expectations, I asked them to identify key issues relating to their ethnicity and personal identity as relevant to academic performance and career choice. The goal was to provide the students the opportunity to situate themselves, reveal bias, gain perspective, and revisit their own concerns around career choice options. The assignment also served as a way to verify the comments I first heard in the initial discussions with the students and provide me with baseline data from which to note their evolution through the research process.

We agreed that each student would be responsible for interviewing at least eight individuals, translating when necessary and transcribing the data. In the end, they conducted a total of fifty-two interviews with Asian Americans in various California settings including San Francisco, Sacramento, San Jose, and Los Angeles. In addition to the interviews, they wrote a reflective statement on each interview commenting on both its authenticity and how it spoke to them. The project took six months. We met every other week during this period to discuss the process and the content of the interviews as we simultaneously developed and considered theories. Based on the interviews with the nine students and comments from their personal essays, I created a list of most frequently stated reasons for not going into teaching and compared them with my previous findings with Asian American teachers. The students verified the accuracy of these reasons based on their own experiences within the Asian American communities. This list was then used as a springboard for developing the interview questions that they used in their research, and, later, in coding the information provided by their informants.

During the first few months of the research, the group reviewed the content and process of the data collection, discussing the following issues: what was emerging, as new, as constant? how to access more information from the interviews? how to expand and refine the interview questions? who else to included and why? Based on the main themes that emerged from these conversations with the researchers, their written reflections, and pilot interviews, I developed an analytical scheme that reflected the salient issues emerging from the process. The scheme allowed for the tracking of variation and consistency across time, population, and region. In comparing what we found as interesting (and therefore discussed among ourselves) with the popularity of responses among the informants, we included frequency of accounts and reasons given for not entering the field of teaching.

As a group we read and matched our coding across all interviews threading back to check for possible cultural misinterpretations and noting paradoxes. We constantly reminded ourselves of the complexity of Asian American identity, noting each informant's current age as well as time of arrival in the United States; conditions of leaving and arriving; parental status in home country in contrast to current occupation; and obvious factors such as country of origin, spoken languages, and gender. Team members understood the problems of operating within the context of the socially constructed rubric of Asian American. We all knew the historical context of antipathy among various Asian groups and especially among Chinese groups: Taiwanese and Mainland Chinese, Hong Kong and other "overseas" Chinese. All of us spoke one or more of the native languages and could compare linguistic variation when discussing in-group/out-group pressures. This commonality of understanding greatly increased our effectiveness in coding and enabled us to look candidly at the complexity and sensitivity of the research results.

Overlaying cultural differences is the historical legacy that each group carries in the form of memories and stories passed down through family and community concerning relations among Asian peoples. Cambodian and Vietnamese, Korean and Japanese, Chinese and Japanese, Vietnamese and Chinese have all been caught in the role of exploiter and victim, predator and prey. Stereotypes and expectations arose around these social constructs, not only with the informants but also with the student interviewers themselves. We realized quickly that if these issues were not revisited and discussed openly, a form of calcification could result. At the start, my students were just as tentative about each other as their grandparents may have been thirty or fifty years ago. To bring them together as a group we had to deconstruct the images of the past to make room for the information that they would be expected to share from their interviews, information which might restimulate old hatreds and animosity.

Most of the student researchers and their informants were unaware that there was a shortage of Asian American public school teachers. This was due to several factors. Most of the researchers grew up in ethnic enclaves where the presence of Asians of common ancestry was strong. Some worked in ethnically based bilingual or community educational programs that employed Asian instructors. In their youth, some attended Saturday Asian identity schools. And last, they did not subscribe to the assumption that race-matched teaching is either better or necessary. Having an Asian teacher in public school did not, from their perspective, assist in their access to knowledge or guarantee their academic or social success. The experience of dialogue through interviewing allowed the student researchers to explore issues of identity and educational achievement within their own social, cultural, and ethnic communities while developing a broader context for their own decision to become teachers.

The interviews provided opportunities for them to talk to people about issues that normally remained hidden or silenced among Asian Americans. A few had some of their first adult conversations with members of their community about career aspirations. Several discovered that family members had been teachers "back home." One student discovered that he came from a long line of prestigious educators back in the Philippines. Some informants revealed how they had been treated when they came to the United States and how they were not seen as professionals, unable to obtain work in an area which they had come to see as their "calling." Conversations that had never occurred before revealed a strong support of, and confusion over, teaching as a profession in this country. As my students explained their understanding of the K–12 system and the shortage of Asian American teachers in assisting in shaping the lives of young people and policies that affect this country, the researchers themselves moved closer to a career commitment to teaching. They also gained the blessing of their families, something which in Asian communities, we found out, is essential if one is to make career moves outside of the prescribed norm of the community. Again the dialogical process of gathering data, providing data, personal transformation and "other" transformation provided unexpected outcomes for everyone involved. The findings were fascinating, complex, and paradoxical (Gordon, 2000b).

Having student researchers explore the reasons why students from similar ethnic backgrounds appeared to be resisting teaching as a profession provided me with insights that I could not have gained otherwise in my own research. First, these students brought enthusiasm to the work; they were considering teaching as a career and wanted to find out why others similar to them were not becoming teachers. Second, as Asian American students closely tied to their respective communities, they had easy access to the population under study. Third, student involvement in research proved fundamental to their academic and professional development. By interviewing other Asian Americans about the choice of teaching as a career, the student researchers provided and provoked thoughtful discussion on critical educational issues, gained insights into aspects of their culture previously left unquestioned, and increased their commitment to the teaching profession.

LATINA IDENTITY: COLLEGES AS SETTINGS FOR CONFUSION

In the same undergraduate course, several Latina students produced powerful essays expressing their difficulty in adjusting to university life, not because of academics or minority status on a predominantly White campus, but because of the pressure imposed on them by their Latina peers to define themselves narrowly and choose acquaintances carefully. While most of them had attempted to conform to these requirements during their first two or three years, now in their senior year, they were questioning what they had gained. Silent, at least at the beginning, in a class of almost a hundred students, their anger and confusion spilled over into their essays and "freewrites." My comments on their written work provoked office visits from some of them, while I spoke with others after and before class. Gradually, I came to learn of the constraints placed on them and how this was impeding their academic achievement in terms of interacting with other students, faculty, and the larger community, including, at times, their extended family.

As our conversations continued, I shared with each of them individually that some of the issues that they perceived as unique to themselves not only were more widespread than they believed but were worthy of further exploration. I invited them to participate in a small research project with me whereby they would conduct interviews with other Latinas who may be struggling with matters of identity. I then suggested that the work might be most productive if those interested in the project worked as a group to share findings and resources. There was far more hesitation at this point, but eight of them agreed. While all were of Mexican heritage except one from Colombia, they varied widely in their point of origin, socioeconomic class, and number of generations of U.S. residency. One was indigenous to Oaxaca. One was mixed race, with a "White" mother and Mexican father but was raised by her father and his family. Three were second-generation American, three were first-generation, and two were immigrants. Variation also existed in the circumstances and schooling of the students and their families; two had college educated parents, but the majority of parents had received minimum education in Mexico. Those parents who had higher education in the United States were professionals while most parents with minimal formal education held working-class jobs, often more than one.

For these Latinas, while geographic and political orientations may have created distance, demarcation lines were far more clearly drawn around socioeconomic status and phenotype. At the beginning, students who had come from migrant families questioned those who had never labored with their hands and their backs. The lighter-skinned students were made to feel as if their skin privilege were something awarded to them rather than inherited. Even though these students knew that within many Latino families the color of the children can range from "White" to "Black" and all hues between, still there was little forgiveness. The grandparents' favoritism toward the fairer child while dismissing "la negrita" remained as painful at twenty years of age as it did at three. Those who suffered familial discrimination took great pains to remind the rest of us of the many ways this has reverberated through their lives.

The campus offered these students a mixture of ethnic-based activities and groups, including student organizations, identity residences, sororities, academic programs, and the usual flow of informal contacts. In general, there were efforts designed to recruit and support Latina/o students in their university work. As with all students, the role of informal grouping proved to be a crucial factor in college success. It has been assumed that ethnic-based programs that facilitated such grouping would have similar results. The picture that emerged, however, in this study and a few related studies (Gordon, 1997a; Duster, 1991) was not altogether encouraging. When the informal group activities are related to academic work and to the professional goals of the students, the results are clearly positive (Astin, 1993; Pace, 1979), but when the informal grouping carries with it tensions associated with home communities and/or asks for loyalty to group identities that have only marginal academic content, students can find themselves more distracted and discouraged in their studies than helped.

The women met with me on a regular basis, biweekly, for six months. I introduced them to basic qualitative research methods: identification of informants, interview protocol, sensitivity and confidentiality when conducting difficult dialogues. To provide them with a critical lens, with time and space for reflection, and to acknowledge any biases they might have, I asked them to write an extensive essay on how the issues about which they were to conduct research had impacted them. These essays served as a springboard for future discussions as well as a way for me to understand their respective contexts. Since the main thrust of the essays related to their perception that their identity was constantly being questioned, we decided to begin the research with the general question: "Latina identity: Who decides what is authentic in which context?" The overall context for the process was a concern for improving the persistence and success of women university students from Spanish/Mexican backgrounds. They explored the hypothesis that social ostracization based on ethnic identity contributes to the thwarting of academic success. In other words, how can a major university present women students from the rich array of Latin cultures with overly simplified and counterproductive choices for being ethnically acceptable within the campus community?

As a group they decided that their research would be of most use to them, and they would be more inclined to put in their best effort if the areas that they undertook for research directly related to concerns and frustrations they had personally experienced. As a result, we came up with three distinct but related topics: the imposition of an identity, the primacy of phenotype in determining authenticity, and the correlation of loss of language with loss of culture. Then we came up with a set of interview questions and probes that would lead most effectively to a greater understanding of the particular topic under investigation.

This project was quite different from the one I engaged in with the Asian American students. In this project while we all shared in the planning and processes, the interview questions were different depending on the research topic that was chosen. Based on their research question, each student set out to identify and then interview individuals who each thought might be struggling with similar concerns. Over the course of six months the students interviewed a total of sixty-three women of Spanish/Mexican heritage. They also transcribed and translated their own tapes or field notes. Our biweekly discussions centered around their increased understanding of the issues; how informants responded to them; as well as the process of data collection. The interviews provided the women with opportunities for them to talk to people about issues that normally remained hidden or silenced among Latinas. As Veronica noted, "I used to feel so isolated until I did this research. I didn't know any of these people before; now they are all friends."

Identity imposition. The greatest irritant that these women expressed upon coming to university was the demand to claim a name, a label—usually not the one they had assumed prior to university life and one which was often at odds with that claimed by their family. Many stated that they resented having an identity imposed upon them based on their looks, their language, or their name. The choices of Mexican, Mexicana, Mexican American, Latina, Chicana, and/or American did not reflect the complexity of who they were; each choice seemed to demarcate affiliation and seemed negative. Some felt that arguments of who was more "real" or who could speak for whom and within what contexts were confining and parochial. They had come to the university to expand their associations, their knowledge, their options for a future; instead, they found themselves trapped in groups that were determined to stifle their newfound freedom.

Realizing that their identity was being socially constructed at the university, some claimed that they had never even thought of labeling themselves prior to coming to college. Most had either grown up in a large Mexican community where being Latino was not claimed as an identity ("I don't want a label; I'm just Letty"), or they grew up in predominantly White communities and had little consciousness of race because they passed as White or were middle-class. ("It just wasn't an issue.")

Phenotype and appearance. The unofficial university definition of what it meant to be authentically Latina/Chicana appeared to be synonymous with that of a stereotypical Mexican migrant farmworker. These images included dark skin, dark hair, dark eyes, relatively short and squat stature, fluency in spoken working-class Spanish, and low socioeconomic status. Some of the student researchers and their informants fit parts of this image but many did not, yet they were all Latina. Preoccupation with appearance and language dominated our discussions. Stories emerged from the interviews that showed college women distorted and distracted. Several of them admitted to severe scarring of their bodies to become acceptable. They did not want the "White college girl" image but rather a new standard, "the California girl," the Chicana. One of the student researchers admitted to wearing brown contacts to cover her blue-green eyes and dying her red hair black to "pass." Actually, the dying of light hair to be "more Mexican" was fairly common as were visits to tanning salons for those who could afford it. A light skinned interviewee explained how "my roommates watched my every move to see how Latina I was."

Language. How well one speaks a language can sometimes determine with whom one speaks it. In the research we repeatedly found students embarrassed by either their lack of fluency in Spanish or their inappropriate accent. As a result, many of them either simply did not speak Spanish with their peers or distanced themselves from other Latinos so as not to be exposed. In a few cases the ridicule and over correction from fluent Spanish speakers and/or university staff/professors was so great that students dropped classes, avoided contact with professors, or began associating with non-Latinos. One student who had done so throughout high school and opted to "hang with Filipinos" arrived at university unsure of how to interact with college-age Latinas. There were numerous stories in which it was assumed, on the one hand, that if you "looked Latina," you could speak Spanish fluently and, on the other hand, if you did not "look Latina," you could not speak Spanish well. As one of the student researchers proclaimed, "People act as if language is a phenotype. Since when does being brown provide you with the linguistic capacity to speak Spanish?"

We found that accent affected identification as well as the willingness of an individual to speak. This was compounded for students who did not speak Spanish fluently and had heavy Mexican accents. These were more often second-generation Americans who had been raised in Mexican-American communities and had never been to Mexico. Some of these students claimed that they had lived in such isolation from English-speaking students that "my first contact with Whites wasn't until college. My school was 95 percent Mexican and 5 percent Black." For some, accent appeared as a signifier for culture. The concern with identity, authenticity, language are combined in this student's comment: "I don't want to speak good English for fear of being consumed by mainstream U.S. and then tempted to leave my community."

College-home tensions. The women in this study, all of Spanish-Mexican descent, often faced contradictory messages and expectations from male partners, families, and communities. Parental pride in their daughter's academic accomplishments was tinged with fear that education would remove her from an eligible pool of partners. Fathers, in particular, were appalled by attitudinal changes of their daughters. When they returned home for holidays or school breaks, the daughters challenged paternal authority and refused to serve the men in ways to which the men were accustomed. They questioned issues of abuse, alcoholism, authoritarianism, and even religion. While wanting to hold on to their "culture" since they perceived that as adding to their authenticity back at college, the women reevaluated the cost of maintaining "culture" if it meant loss of self. The struggles between the group and the individual hit first-generation college students the hardest as their dream had been to return to their community to live and work. Parents, wanting some visible results from college, were often left confused by discussions of majors that held no apparent relationship to a job. The longer the women stayed at college, the harder it was for them to imagine returning home.

Affiliation and partnering. The vast majority of these women, regardless of socioeconomic class, opted for serious relationships with men who were not as academically grounded as they. Most were "going with" men who had little knowledge of the demands of university life and assumed the women's academic interests were a passing phase. A few of the men were taking courses part-time at community college; others had never been on a college campus. The men expected the women to marry and have children immediately following baccalaureate graduation. Clearly this would confound the chances for the woman to pursue advanced degree work or obtain a satisfying job commensurate with her talents. It would also make her somewhat dependent on the partner who, in most cases, had a laboring job and had no inclination or aspiration to move out of such work. In discussions with these women, the student researchers and I, who knew of the possibility of being trapped in the same cycle, consistently found that the Latinas were totally cognizant of the situation but unable to see how they could move out of it. The fear of not finding husbands was almost paralyzing. Some claimed to want to have "five or six kids and before I am too old to enjoy them. It's a part of my dream."

I was particularly intrigued by the resistance for these women to date college-educated Latinos. Although there were several intelligent, attractive, and interesting Latinos in the class and around campus in general, they were not seen as potential partners with these Latinas. When I inquired about some of these men, whom I knew quite well because of their work with me as research assistants or in my classes, I was told that they were not exciting enough. Alicia, one of the many academically sound students with a bright future ahead of her, told me, "The guys here on campus are too academic. I want a guy to have fun with." She said to me that she was running with a "low rider," who was unemployed and hated by her parents. It was as if men who chose to come to university somehow lost their allure as real men. Given that several of these men were also interested in becoming educators and working in their communities, the loss was doubly painful. Were we somehow perpetuating the stereotype that has plagued schools for years, that men interested in working with children or youth are somehow less male and therefore suspect?

GANG AFFILIATION AND EDUCATIONAL ASPIRATIONS

The following are accounts about two of my students.

Four foot eight, flashing eyes, red nails and skimpy clothes with a cocky air, she exuded defiance and demanded space. She hung with the Latinos but loosely so. Primed for a fight, her curiosity got the better of her as she ventured into my office after class one day. She wanted to know how I knew what I did about the issues being discussed in class. She wanted to share, as I had done, something about her life. They had called her "killer" as she set about to prove to her peers within Los Angeles gang culture that despite, or perhaps because of, her mixed heritage (African American and Mexican) she should be accepted. Arriving in this country at age twelve after five of her brothers had died in a fire back in Mexico, she struggled to gain some respect. School had been a battlefield.

Juan was declared illiterate at age fourteen. Having left home to save himself from his alcoholic and drug-addicted parents, he worked full time while trying to stay in school. Gangs were just a part of the scenery. His family belonged to gangs; he was born into them. "La familia" crossed international borders, making the profit margin a temptation even to someone who was trying to stay out of the flow. He ended up in prison where he learned to read and received his GED. Five years later he was in my class.

Urban youth gangs as a factor in college achievement are a neglected area of educational research. Gang culture is no longer something that is left in the streets. It has permeated life in California to such a degree that a large proportion of urban youth is affected by it whether by choice or by circumstances. Given the prevalence of gang affiliation among our youth, it should come as no surprise that some of these young people are not only successful high school students but are moving into prestigious universities and colleges. The work reported here documents the process by which students identified themselves as gang members, the author's interviews with them, and their induction into an ethnographic research project whereby they interviewed other gang members and people who had been affected by, or associated with, gangs. The purposes were three-fold: (1) to enable college students who perceived themselves as marginalized because of their gang affiliation to make the linkage between their past and present; (2) to deconstruct the assumptions around gang affiliation and the reasons for gang membership; and (3) to explore the role of academics in gang life.

While teaching the course "Minorities and the Schooling Process" above, I realized that I had at least seven gang members in the class (seven had declared themselves). I came to find out there were more who had been radically affected by gangs, losing a brother, a father, a friend, a lover. The disclosures came as a result of readings and discussions on urban education. All students in the class were to select a research topic of interest to them. Several, including many middle-class, nonurban-educated students, chose "violence and gangs" as their topic. As the rough drafts for the paper began to dribble in after the first two weeks of the quarter, I realized that even though middle-class white students were citing research, their assumptions about the causes of violence and gangs did not fit with some of the stories I had heard from the students who had spoken to me about their gang affiliation.

To many of the middle-class students, a gang member was someone who was from a low-income, broken home who had no supervision and a family that could care less about his or her education or future. This was not the case, however, for about half of the students who had spoken to me about their gang experience. I felt that the best education I could provide for the class would be if the students who had spoken to me could share some of their experience with the class. Five of them agreed. One day we held a "fish-bowl" class session whereby the five students sat in the center of the classroom and spoke to each other about a range of issues that they had discussed with me individually. The rest of the class, about seventy-five students that day, circled around, sitting or standing to hear. The testimonies and revelations were powerful and painful. The class response ranged from shock to disbelief. Most had never imagined the lives some of these students had lived. As a result of this forum, many of the observing students questioned the assumptions that most of the media and the academic literature profess. A few who had researched violence and gangs for their final paper wanted to start over, beginning with more in-depth interviews with their peers who had been a part of gangs. They did not get anywhere with this idea but I acknowledged the validity of their reasoning and decided to pursue it on a different level.

Having gone through this disclosure and realizing even more vividly the discrepancy between their lives "back home" and their college existence, I invited those students who had either participated in the forum or who had had contact with gangs to begin the process of bridging these two worlds. Seven students, three males and four females, all Latino, agreed to the project, which lasted about one year. Prior to commencing the interviews with their friends, families, and associates, the student researchers wrote extensively on their life experiences and what affected their decision to move toward academic success and hence their arrival at a major research university. Moreover, they wrote about gang affiliation in an academic context. Part of their "write-up" for each interview related their own views on how authentic the recounting was, how the respondent perceived them and how the conversation affected their own understanding of their past and present.

The seven student researchers conducted fifty-seven interviews about the interaction between gang involvement and academic achievement before and during college. Much of the work was translated from Spanish, some remained in Spanglish. Research sites included Los Angeles, Sacramento, Salinas, Watsonville, and San Jose. We met once a month, as these interviews were more difficult to acquire. Initially, the dialogue among the student researchers proved difficult due to issues of trust. For some, it was a matter of safety, for others, life and death.

The research process was designed to reconnect marginalized youth who had been unable to make a link between their past affiliation with gang culture and their current collegial life. As a result of the work, these students were able to integrate the many phases of their lives and come out of "hiding." They realized that their expertise and knowledge were important resources for educators who work with youth and for a greater understanding of the culture. The students gained extensive ethnographic research training that enabled them to perceive themselves for the first time as potential scholars rather than college students. All of these students intended to go on to graduate school. The results from the work provide a basis for interpretations of college experience for former youth gang members and of educational perceptions and aspirations among a sample of college-age participants in urban gangs. The research process offers one example of how critical ethnography can add significantly to teacher preparation in a diverse undergraduate cohort.

This chapter illustrates how ethnographic research pedagogy creates opportunities for increased awareness of students' multiple identities. Without an understanding of the complexity of the lives of youth, educators blindly create ineffective programs or place students at risk. I seek to create a shift in the "political" landscape of higher education, especially teacher preparation, as educators ask about and listen to the experience of those they serve.

CHAPTER 2

Immigrants and Education: Dialogic Inquiry as Pedagogy

DIALOGUE BETWEEN STUDENTS AND MEMBERS OF IMMIGRANT COMMUNI-
ties, including their own families, can provide a transformative
pedagogy that works to create new meanings within and along-
side the institutions and traditions that young people face in
their life choices. The goal of my work as an educator is a dialogue conducted and discovered within a critical interpretation
of the circumstances in which we live, an approach that shares
the goals of Michrina and Richards in their book *Person to Person: Fieldwork, Dialogue, and the Hermeneutic Method* (1996).
The undergraduate course discussed in this chapter attempted
to enhance student success by having a cohort of diverse students work in collaboration with each other, their family, and
the wider community—a community they may never have considered before.

Creating situations in which future teachers and other undergraduate college students can broaden their understanding
of the complexity of the immigrant experience has intrigued me
for years. As an educator in California focused on urban and immigrant issues, I have been as concerned that my Latino students understand the lives of Cambodian and Samoan children
as I have been that my White students of non-Hispanic descent
understand the challenges facing immigrant children of color. As
a college student, it is easy to assume, particularly if you are an
immigrant or first-generation American, that you understand
the forces that compel people to emigrate from another country

to the United States. It is also easy to slip into the mindset that most Latinos and Asians, categories socially constructed for American consumption, are either immigrants or have retained what has been called an immigrant world view. Similarly, immigrant students whose skin is "White" are often invisible and their needs ignored. Many of these "White" individuals come from countries that are radically different from the United States; some are refugees, some have received little schooling, and many do not speak English.

As one of several interdisciplinary undergraduate courses offered by a university department of education, "Immigrants and Education" examined the economic, political, and social motivations as well as the aspirations and attitudes that immigrants bring to the United States and to their negotiation with American schooling. The goals of the course were:

1. to examine our own beliefs and mythologies about immigrants and attempt to understand the differences among and between apparently similar "groups" of individuals;
2. to examine critically a variety of research literature on immigrants;
3. to consider the practical applications of this research for the education of immigrant children and the inclusion of their communities in a discussion on education; and
4. to engage students in field research inquiring into immigrants' experiences adapting to American schooling.

The premise of the course was learning from dialogue with immigrants. The lectures, guest speakers, films, readings, and discussion addressed the causes, motivations, and consequences of immigration from a global perspective within a historical analysis that provided a context for understanding conflict among immigrant groups and between immigrants and national minorities as well as suggesting approaches to teaching culturally and linguistically diverse students. After preparatory training exercises, students conducted face-to-face interviews with immigrants in order to confront myths and develop an awareness of present-day dilemmas and decisions pertaining to education among and within immigrant groups. Reflective writing throughout the course asked for an examination of preconceptions before the interviews and interpretations gained through the interviews. Research papers looked in depth at immigration from one country while small group performances attempted to capture the lives of immigrants from widely varied areas of the world.

While the course material included consideration of internal migration within the United States, specifically that of African Americans moving north and west from the South as well as other rural to urban movement, the interviews were exclusively with immigrant groups from outside the United States. The readings for the course included *California's Immigrant Children* (Rumbaut & Cornelius, 1995) and *The Inner World of the Immigrant Child* (Igoa, 1995), as well as excerpts from *Educating Immigrant Children: Schools and Language Minorities in Twelve Nations* (Glenn and De Jong, 1996), *Growing Up American: How Vietnamese Children Adapt to Life in the United States* (Zhou & Bankston, 1998), and *Minority Status and Schooling: A Comparative Study of Immigrant and Involuntary Minorities* (Gibson & Ogbu, 1991). Throughout the quarter, guest speakers from several nations (e.g., Vietnam, Russia, China, India, Ethiopia, and El Salvador) told their own stories; students had the opportunity to interrogate them on a range of issues such as teaching one's home language of Mandarin to your three-year-old daughter as well as the humiliation of seeing your father, who had been a lawyer in Vietnam, reduced to poverty and eking out a living of emptying coins from slot machines in Las Vegas.

Of the nearly eighty students in the course, the majority of students were within two generations of the immigrant experience and those were mostly Mexican Americans and Asian Americans; there were also students of Central American, Latin American, and recent European and African origin as well. While the largest group of students in class appeared to be "White," we soon found out how "whiteness," while granting privilege in majority situations, also erased the visible cues often used in an effort to receive some understanding of the struggles against racism and nativism. The list of "White" students who themselves were immigrants or first-generation Americans and who had been raised in traditional ethnic homes far exceeded the number of "White" students who saw themselves as "just American without any culture." The ethnically identified White students included not only "White" Latinos from Mexico, Columbia, Panama, Chile, and Argentina but also students from Italy, Hungary, Greece, Russia, Poland, Sweden, and Israel as well as Canada, Ireland, and the United Kingdom.

THE INTERVIEWING PROCESS

I introduce students to my form of dialogic inquiry with a discussion of the interview process as an interaction based on trust. I stress the importance of listening to each other, resisting the imposition of your ideas or authority, and allowing yourself to be informed and your assumptions challenged. A beginning exercise involves a simple partnership in which each student shares something about herself or himself that others would not know about them just from observation. A further step asks students to share with another partner the misperceptions that people have had about them. A short in-class writing early in the course asks students to name a cultural identifier that they think others do not know about their own culture or a culture with which they are familiar.

As stated above, interviews with immigrants serve as the backbone of the course. Each student is required to go into the community to conduct at least four interviews with first- or second-generation immigrants to the United States who are from four different countries. Initially, I had asked that the interviewees not originate from the same country as the student conducting the interview but I later modified the assignment when I discovered how little my students knew of their own family histories. Many had never spoken with their parents, relatives, or community members regarding their arrival to this country or what, and who, was left behind. As a result, one of the four interviews can be with a family member who can share his or her story of coming to terms with American schooling.

The goal of the four interviews was to test students' assumptions against reality as well as provide insight into the similarities among individuals from a variety of cultures who were caught in a common struggle of accommodation to a new environment. The interviews focused on ways in which the immigrants or their parents encountered and adjusted to the American educational system as well as other topics crucial to the immigrant experience. The following were interview questions that the students could adjust when needed:

- How was English learned? (speaking, writing, reading)
- What was supportive, or was not supportive, about the school setting?
- How did schooling challenge and/or reinforce the authority of the family? vice versa?
- Were children expected to work within the family and, if so, did this conflict with demands of schooling?
- How did parents engage the school?
- Were there "identity schools" or churches that served to assist in education and/or acculturation?
- What choices of subject matter and courses grew from family influence?
- What choices were made in preparation for careers?
- Had anyone returned to his or her native country and, if so, how was he or she perceived and treated after having spent time in the United States?

At first many of the students were hesitant. So, after providing them with guidelines, informing them of protocol procedures, and brainstorming possible interview questions that would lead to our goal of understanding educational differences across cultures and negotiation of the American educational system, I had them interview one of their fellow classmates who was from a country different from their own. The pairs usually included one immigrant or child of immigrant parent(s) with one nonimmigrant student. This provided an interviewing experi-

ence that brought the class together as a coherent entity working on a singular project; it also provided contacts with the
larger community outside the classroom as students offered suggestions to one another about whom they might interview.

Each student wrote up a summary and reflection of each of
the four outside-of-class interviews and turned it in each week
prior to beginning the next interview. The process of face-to-face
interviews provided a powerful context for the students to hear
from people who seldom told their stories to Americans or outsiders. The persons interviewed, in turn, were able to inform the
students in ways that I could not. The range of information received as well as the lives touched through the interviews far exceeded my in-class instruction. The role of interviewer assumed
by the students provided the distance and excuse to intervene
and inquire into peoples' lives. The interviewees, however, did
not see it as intrusion; far from it, it became an opportunity to
educate young people (some of whom might be future teachers)
about their culture, aspirations, dreams, struggles, and frustrations with American life and its educational system (McCaleb,
1995; Vella, 1997).

REFLECTIVE WRITING

The interviews provided an opportunity to gather stories from
immigrants of their educational negotiation once in the United
States. They also served as a springboard for other questions related to the contradictions and conflicts that immigrants face
when attempting to return to their country, retain their language, or counteract disabling attitudes toward academic success. While the interview process took place with outside
informants, I wanted students to interrogate simultaneously
their own knowledge base and locate the origins of their biases.
To allow for this process, I asked them to write several short essays of personal reflections and two longer and critical essays
exploring questions with which scholars in the field of immigration and urban studies grapple. I wanted students to see themselves as valid resources of information since many were either
immigrants themselves or from second- and third-generation

immigrant families. This self-reflection, increasingly informed by their interviews, enabled them to place their success at gaining entrance to a major research university within a larger theoretical context; moreover, it assisted them in understanding the multitude of reasons why immigrants respond differentially to schooling (Ogbu, 1991).

The short reflective essay topics included:

1. Write of your experience with immigration, migration, and/or uprootedness. In what ways have you lived in an immigrant community?
2. Write about how you feel about the cultural identity/ identities attributed to you versus how you see yourself. How do you think that you are seen by strangers? by family? by friends?
3. Write about how your cultural identity affected your schooling. How were you aware of race and class as a child?
4. Write about what happens when you return home from the university. How are you perceived and treated?
5. What are your thoughts about what happens when some of the children in a family are born in a home country and some in the United States?

The two in-depth essays considered:

1. How are immigrants perceived and treated when they return to their home country after having spent time in the United States?
2. Based on your work in the course, discuss your agreement or disagreement with the following two statements: (a) Most Mexican Americans want public schools to provide second-language instruction in Spanish for their children whereas most Asian Americans prefer schools to teach in English only, and (b) Mexican Americans value family over education and Asians value education over family.

BACKGROUND RESEARCH

Another major part of the course entailed research of a very different type. To deepen their understanding of the historical context as well as the socioeconomic forces at play in the movement of people to the United States, I required the students to select one of the four countries represented by their interviews for a more thorough investigation. This part of the inquiry included the reading of at least one short story or novel, a biography or autobiography, as well as standard library research work in referred journals and books. Although they could do the research at their own pace, they had to complete a rough draft by week eight of a ten-week quarter in order to participate fully in the development of the next phase of the course, the group performances.

GROUP PERFORMANCES

Midway through the course, after deciding with whom their four interviews would take place, I divided the students into groups representing countries in a common region of the world, regardless of differences in religion, ethnicity, or language, for example, India, Pakistan, and Bangladesh. I required the students to collaborate in developing a performance piece highlighting the unique as well as the common characteristics exemplifying the struggles of immigration and acculturation as based on their interviews. Students got the opportunity to share with two or three peers their newfound knowledge, based on their individual library research and their interviews. They explained the differences and similarities of their chosen country or culture with those of others. They also negotiated an acceptable motif for the group that could enact this understanding for the entire class. The "performances," which took place the last week of classes, ranged from skits to musicals to poetry readings and everything in between. Most included costumes, props, and food.

Because of the diversity represented among the students within the class itself, significant attempts were made to portray accurately individuals and their culture. This required that the students checked with their classmates from the country or cul-

ture they were "performing" but who are not within their prescribed presentation group. By using multiple points of entry
from which to engage over and over again in dispelling preconceptions of immigrants, the process affirmed common struggles
and clarified differences based on educational and socioeconomic
background, country of origin, refugee/immigrant status, language acquisition, religion, age at entry, and gender.

STUDENT RESPONSES TO ESSAY ASSIGNMENTS

In an attempt to give students an opportunity to consider the issues immigrants face in their movement to America and to reflect further on what they had learned thus far in the course, I
asked them to write two essays on the following questions.

1. *How are immigrants perceived and treated when they return to their home country after having spent time in the United
States?*

It was important for the students to realize the power of socialization and acculturation within any society and how that
power affected not only the ability to thrive but survival itself.
Many of the changes we go through by being in another culture,
another country, occur without our awareness of them. In this
exercise I wanted students to *see* this unconscious process
through the eyes of those who had returned "home," often to be
treated a stranger in their own land. As one student wrote, "I became totally aware of identity after returning from Mexico." I
also wanted to give students who had *not* returned to their
"home" a glimpse of the reality that while they may claim to
identify strongly here in the United States with their home
country, they may be perceived as American when they return or
travel "home" for the first time. This experience was even true
for a woman from Ethiopia who had not come to the United
States until age ten. When she visited Ghana at age twenty, she
assumed she would be embraced as a fellow African; instead she
was perceived as an American with no distinction being made
between her and her group of peers who were comprised of
Whites and African Americans. My goal with this controversial

question was to reveal variations in attitudes, to honor changing identities, and to move away from the assumption that individuals with a particular visible ethnic identity have a knowledge of the culture or country from which they are descended.

Most students who evaluated other students' authenticity at university based on their ability to speak the home language found that when they returned "home," they were often ridiculed either for their loss of the language or their lack of fluency. Family and friends found it difficult to understand how they could lose a language. Many faced harsh laughter when speaking Spanish with an American accent. One young Mexicana student commented, "I was embarrassed to speak to others while in Mexico. I went silent. You would not have recognized me." Other demarcations of difference included clothing, make-up, body language, gait, attitude, and lack of respect. Several interviewees spoke of being chastised for dressing in a way that intimated stereotypical gang affiliation, such as baggy pants, bandanas, tattoos. Similarly, deference for others and knowledge of one's position within the family was lost on many of the returnees. "I was seen as too loud; I laughed too much." Lack of an ability to socialize in the same way as family relatives left the returnees with the label of being "stuck up." One interviewee commented, "They think that you look down on them just because you don't act like them."

Educated women were found to be a major target of suspicion, particularly if they were not married or at least under consideration by their twenties or beyond. This latter point provoked commentary from my female students who perceived a double standard. Family members back home were proud of their educational accomplishments but would not let "their girls" continue in their schooling or go to America. As one student stated, "They thought that all people who move to, or are born in, North America eventually become liberal. This was not seen as a positive thing." These perceptions by family members and community back home were as vivid for Chinese as for Indian, Mexican, or Jamaican. The interviewing process made it quite clear that traditional cultures are conservative by nature and that culture is dependent on continuity of patterns and attitudes (Rosaldo, 1989; Geertz, 1973). Leaving home is often an irreversible process for the immigrant and acquiring a new national identity necessarily involves the risk of forgoing one's home culture and identity.

2. Do you agree with the following two statements? (a) Most Mexican Americans want public schools to provide second-language instruction in Spanish for their children whereas most Asian Americans prefer schools to teach in English only, and (b) Mexican Americans value family over education and Asian Americans value education over family.

The two statements originated with remarks made by an elementary school principal who was a guest speaker for the course based on his thirty years of experience with Latino and Asian American students and families. The responses to his generalizations proved insightful both in what a question can pull from students but also in how students will respond in writing but not in public voice. While all students were very cautious about making generalizations in their written responses, there were great differences in views depending on who had had experience with Latino or Asian cultures and who had not. Those who had had contact with either of these groups agreed with the statements or enhanced the assumption along lines I will explain later. Those students who did not have contact or personal relations, mostly those who were middle class, White, and had college educated parents, saw the assumptions as racist generalizations and dismissed them. Ironically, their ranting silenced the students who had first-hand knowledge of family priorities from these cultures.

The points of departure for those who disagreed with the statement about pubic education and who either were Latino or Asian or had had extensive contact with these groups were interesting. Those that disagreed with the assumption chose to alter the assumption by asserting that most Latino parents, in fact, did *not* want the public schools to teach their children about their culture or their language. They claimed that parents saw school as a place for their children to learn about America and how to be successful, stating: "They want public schools to teach

English, not Spanish. Children must be exposed to the 'language of power' which in this country is English." Similarly, clarification on the Asian American side produced some powerful testimonies. While there was agreement that Asian American parents, in general, wanted schools to teach only English to their children, this did not mean that most Asian parents simultaneously maintained what could be considered a "home culture" separate from "American" culture. Rather, for most students their culture had become a montage of the new and the old. The degrees of retention of the home culture were often dependent on which ethnicity we were speaking about, the historical context, and the length of time in the United States. One Japanese student reminded us that "The *few* Japanese Americans I know with a desire to learn the language usually go to Japanese schools on weekends; they don't learn it or speak it at home." He claimed this was true for other "Asian ethnic groups" though I am not sure this applies to newer Southeast Asian groups who may be more inclined to maintain language as a means to communicate with family members and do not have the same history of "Saturday schools" as the Chinese, Japanese, and Korean communities.

While most students thought that both groups value education and family, the Latino students and Latino interviewees overwhelmingly verified the claim that if it were a choice between family and education, family would come first. Often they framed this view in terms of parents' education, time in country, and socioeconomic demands. One female first-generation college student, who at the time of the class had a three-year-old son, wrote, "For myself and my child, two generations have been formed in which I believe education will be as strongly emphasized as family has been in the past." Several students attempted to explain how the assumptions might be true: "Latinos might want their culture and language taught in schools because they fear the government is trying to change them. Asians are sojourners, far from their home country; they see English as beneficial. Latinos are migrants; they may return home and will need the language to do so."

LEARNING FROM THE INTERVIEWS

Generational differences. Student interviewers found signifi-
cance in the variety of ways their interviewees spoke of first-
generations students being "indebted to parents' hardships" or
"honoring parents' struggle." A Korean student's summary said,
"They gave up everything to come to this country." A Salvadorian
student echoed the point, saying, "First-generation students
want to fulfill the goals and dreams that their parents did not
have the chance to attain." Others stated that for first-generation Americans "there is much to prove not only to one's self and
family but to those left behind."

For many students from all ethnic groups, stories of life "back
home," particularly if the leaving was due to economic or political reasons, served as a framework for understanding the immigrants' enthusiasm for the new country and educational
opportunities it could afford. Difficulties with language and a
new culture were often seen by newly arrived immigrants as
barriers to overcome with the assumption that with this success
would come access (Gandara, 1995). For those who gained from
the hard work, overcame the ostensible obstacles, and received
rewards for their efforts through social and economic mobility,
the likelihood of maintaining a positive attitude and high educational aspirations was greater. For the others, the cynicism of a
fading American dream could easily be nurtured in urban enclaves (Massey & Denton, 1993; Sklar, 1995). Several interviewees told poignant versions of the resulting paralysis brought on
by the conflict between wanting to succeed academically and
fearing ostracization by peers and family if they did.

Many interviews made clear that second- and third-
generation youth were not nurtured on the same stories as initial immigrants; they did not share the same struggles nor
shoulder the same responsibilities. As a result, ties to the group
weaken, one's identity begins to evolve as it is simultaneously
contested, and there is increasing concern for fitting in, not
sticking out. To be "ethnic" is often not valued for the second
generation (Bhatti, 1999). Habits of respect that sustain first-

generation Americans, providing them with a demeanor that appeals to teachers, are shed as peer group pressure demands greater independence of thought, action, and word (Davidson, 1996). Schooling, once seen as a privilege, starts to be taken for granted. It is seen as compulsory, a chore rather than a gift. This attitude continues on to postsecondary learning where we see ethnic minority university students, who were born in the United States and have never been to their "home country," claiming a much stronger ethnic identity than recently arrived immigrants, and oftentimes separating themselves from their "brothers and sisters," perceiving their enthusiasm and aspirations for life in America as a rejection of their culture.

Home language. My students found that most interviewees claimed that the main barrier to demonstrating high quality work and accessing knowledge was their lack of fluency in English and the limited number of teachers or counselors who could operate effectively in their home language. This included a shortage of school staff sensitive to variation of language and cultures across arbitrarily demarcated spaces. For example, not all arriving from Mexico speak Spanish; some may be indigenous peoples who speak their own language. And even for those who do speak Spanish, one cannot assume that they write or read it. However, to operate out of the assumption that immigrants from Mexico are migrant workers or that they have not had formal education is to reinforce naiveté and ignorance of a very complex, highly sophisticated country and culture (Shorris, 1992). Similarly, "Asian" people represent a range of languages, religions, ethnicities, and cultures as well as levels of education, socioeconomic class, and familiarity with urban contexts. Even Chinese people, ostensibly an identifiable ethnic group, speak various languages and dialects, depending on where they live, many of which are incomprehensible to other Chinese people (Takaki, 1989).

Disappointment with U.S. educational system. Shocking as many students found it to be, many of their interviews revealed that for those individuals who are privileged to be educated "back home," wherever that may be, schooling in America was perceived as less academic, not as rigorous, as that in their own country. This finding is not new, as Gougeon (1993) and others have discussed it at length, but for undergraduates who have been reared to see the United States as number one, this new information was indeed startling, particularly when it was confirmed by some of the immigrant student stories in the class. Several interviews revealed that individuals who had taken advanced math or science "back home" found themselves placed in "basic" courses here in the United States because of local ignorance about other educational systems and the linguistic limitations of students, parents, and teachers as well as the hesitancy on the part of many immigrant parents to question or contradict the authority of the school. Other interviewees who as children migrated back and forth to Mexico highlighted their placement in much more challenging classes at higher grade levels in Mexico while residing there compared with their placements in the United States. Their return to the United States often meant sitting through boring, redundant classes one or two levels below the work done in Mexico. Older children often reacted to this situation by dropping out due to the frustration. Younger children just fell farther and farther behind. The waste in terms of human potential was obvious to the student interviewers.

Many of the changes we go through by being in another culture, another country, occur without our knowledge. It is important for students to realize the power of socialization and acculturation within any society, not only to survive, but to thrive. Many of my students spoke in dismay of the strong educational aspirations of immigrants as well as their focus, as reflected in this student's comment regarding an Ethiopian he interviewed: "To Samson, education comes first; he does not party; he takes his curriculum very seriously. Samson takes care of his business before anything else." This was said of a student who, like other African, European, and Asian immigrants, entered the United States through Canada, oftentimes without any family members or with only a few. In this case, the father had to stay behind. The U.S. students revealed a complacency about their schooling that speaks clearly of their first-world privilege, whatever their immigrant or ethnic heritage.

Those who did *not* have the opportunity of an education prior to arriving in the United States had mixed feelings toward compulsory schooling until the age of sixteen. In most countries, depending on one's socioeconomic background, education beyond middle school is a privilege; it is not compulsory as it is in the United States. This is true in developed countries such as Japan and England as well as in economically challenged spaces like equatorial regions of Africa and South America. Elementary education is perceived as providing most people with the rudimentary skills necessary for survival. Young people are often needed to assist the family financially. This is not child labor, as our interviews showed us, but reality. Some of the interviewees argued that such cooperative work relations actually heighten family cohesion and provide greater employment opportunities and networking than the distancing that can occur with the severing of ties to the community when one leaves for "higher education."

Some Eastern European interviewees noted that young men who had come to America at age sixteen, after they had completed their formal education "back home" were insulted by the assumption that they should return to school, particularly if the quality and level of their education in their home country exceeded that of the school they were to enter in the United States. Back home they had already assumed responsibility for their families, had worked jobs, and had been given the freedom to live as an adult complete with permission to drink and smoke in public without fear of reprisal. To be treated as a child in U.S. public schools, after having made the decision to immigrate to America, was a difficult, if not impossible, task. A few of these individuals calculated the costs and opted to bypass the last few years of high school and go directly to community college and, as a result, jump-start their college education by two years at an affordable price. The cumulative result for the student interviewers was a much wider view of how American schooling stands in relationship to that of other nations.

Common beliefs. One of the most surprising findings for the students was that immigrants, in general, no matter if they were from Africa, Asia, Europe, or the Americas, tended to have similar experiences in adjusting to life in this country (Rumbaut & Cornelius, 1995). There were concerns about the widening generational gap that inevitably happens with time spent in the new country and about the difficulty adjusting to a new language and culture (often accompanied by the loss or modification of one's home language and culture). There was also confusion about, and at times disappointment with, the American educational system, which maintains education as a birthright and not as a privilege (Ogbu & Simons, 1998).

The vast majority of the immigrant interviewees, to the surprise of my students, held to a common belief structure, regardless of the ostensible differences in countries, which could, by American standards, be considered conservative. This included a hesitancy toward strangers, a protective attitude toward their young, a belief that strict discipline is essential, a powerful work ethic, reverence toward elders, respect for education and teachers, and high expectations for their children. Ironically, my students came to see the United States as the anomaly. There was something about life in America that worked against these traits, particularly in large urban areas (Gordon, 2000a; Ogbu, 1995; Suarez-Orozco, 1991). Most immigrants were caught between excitement about greater opportunities in the new land and fear that their children would be swallowed up by the shallow, but deadly, competition for attention and resources. Many felt that life back home was safer and simpler and provided more time for family and friends. My students found the sharing of these feelings sobering.

CONCLUSION

The "Immigrants and Education" course served to inform, enlighten, and transform attitudes of all students regardless of their immigrant status. Americans know little of the political and economic forces that drive and/or deter schooling globally. They are unaware that for many other societies schooling is a privilege, not a right. Hence, students from many countries who *do have* the opportunity for formal schooling not only place a high value on education but carry the added burden of being rep-

resentatives of their village or town. The urgency of economic
and cultural survival for marginalized groups within U.S. society can impede their willingness to explore the complexity of the
international community and how it impacts their daily lives.
This is particularly true when international issues are sepa-
rated from multicultural concerns. Often, culturally isolated
students, particularly from the working-class, perceive interna-
tionalization as a threat. The response to the perceived threat is
often ethnocentric with strong racial overtones. Without the
knowledge of the larger forces that determine economic, social,
and political stratification in this society, the cycle of one ethnic
group oppressing another continues. Competition for jobs is particularly intense for those whose education has been limited,
whether they be Americans or recent immigrants. Used by cor-
porate and political leaders to suppress strikes and collaboration
among workers, ethnic infighting has a long history. A lack of
global perspective leads to the assumption that America is
unique in its ethnic issues.

Lack of knowledge of other cultures and of immigrants' experiences fuels disrespect and assumes people of other origins do
not have a history worth honoring (Gillborn, 1990). Many immigrants come from cultures that have endured for thousands of
years. They have traditions, religions, and belief systems from
which Americans could learn. Clearly, the inability to speak
English fluently is not the only indicator of one's value to his or
her community, especially an American community. Yet, Americans continue to hesitate to embrace multiculturalism and mul-
tilingualism as assets, preferring to see them as deficits or
problems to be overcome. Students from diverse language backgrounds along with their parents and community are not seen as
"funds of knowledge" who could enhance the quality of the curriculum (Moll, 1990). The role of cross-cultural study must be informed by the needs of all American students, including the
overcoming of cultural parochialism due to racial and cultural
isolation as well as inadequate schooling.

CHAPTER 3

Future Teachers Assist in Urban, Low-Income, Multicultural Classrooms

WHILE STUDENTS CHOSE MY PRE-PROFESSIONAL COURSES IN EDUCATION with some level of commitment to teaching, that commitment was usually tentative and almost always untested and uninformed. As I introduced them to low-income, urban classrooms, I meant to inquire into their assumptions and expand on their prior knowledge. In the process, I wanted to induce the transformation of their commitment so that it would mature and grow to meet the challenges of urban classroom teaching (Haberman, 1996; O'Loughlin & Campbell, 1988). In constructing a transformative pedagogy, I sought to combine various approaches within the constraints of university class sizes from 20 to 280 and with students from all majors and at all levels of college work.

In sending students into urban classrooms, I asked more than the usual observation or tutoring. In addition, I prepared and expected them to carry out the tasks of ethnography: observation of the larger educational context both inside and outside of the classroom, including the overall school setting, the surrounding community, and religious institutions. They also conducted interviews with other students and teachers and gave an interpretation of the students' lives as seen through the school experience. Through a variety of means, I prepared them for work as ethnographers with a critical perspective, that is, I expected them to make connections between the sometimes harsh realities of the classroom and the even harsher conditions of life faced by many low-income minority and immigrant families.

The fieldwork took place in a school district of fourteen elementary and middle schools serving 11,000 students, of which 48 percent were Latino, 38 percent Asian, mostly Vietnamese and Cambodians, 6 percent African American, and the remainder, Whites and mixed race. Eighty-five percent of the students were on free or reduced lunch. Most students were not proficient in English. In contrast, most of the teachers who taught in these schools claimed to have been unprepared to work with the student population. My purpose in setting up this situation was to provide a venue in which my undergraduate students could assist teachers by tutoring students in need, while also engaging teachers, staff, and students in both formal interviews and informal conversations that would illuminate my students' understanding of the school and community.

The title of the course was "Race, Class, and Culture in Education." The course examined the culture of schooling through an exploration of socialization, marginalization, and assimilation. The readings for the course included *Facing Racism in Education* (Hidalgo, McDowell, & Siddle, 1993), *City Kids, City Teachers*, (Ayers & Ford, 1996), and *Ain't No Making It: Leveled Aspirations in a Low-income Neighborhood* (MacLeod, 1987), as well as a wide variety of articles. While the readings focused on the factors that impede or support the academic success of students of color and working-class students, I asked my undergraduates to embrace the complexity of multiple identities and move away from categorical mindsets. I asked them to be attentve to "masks of normality" and myths of at-riskness and to give a critical look at the "majority" model of schooling and socialization. We explored how socioeconomic class intersects with "race" and how "culture," while not the only determining characteristic, serves as a powerful predisposition for one's orientation to education. Guest speakers, especially administrators and principals from the district, played an important role in providing realistic scenarios and information about the district and the schools in which the undergraduates were working. The course involved a combination of lectures, student presentations, discussions, small group activities, in-class writing, and fieldwork. All students had the opportunity to present a chapter or article from the readings to the class once during the quarter. This was done in small groups where they prepared ahead of time a format that would enhance and elaborate on what they had read. Often, skits, musicals, and posters emerge from this work.

A different set of groupings took place around their research/interviews in the schools. After generating a list of issues of particular importance to urban contexts and narrowing this down to about eight topics, the students selected one of these as the theme of the research they would conduct in one of ten schools in the district. The group of students assigned to a specific school was selected so that each student had a different research topic. There were ten groups of about eight students with each of the eight students in the same school looking at a different research topic.

A representative list of research topics suggested for the course included:

1. Life plans and aspirations, career interests. What do students want to be? How do teacher expectations help or hinder students' aspirations in general or plans of specific individuals?
2. Student affiliation. What groups are observed informally and what groups are provided by structured programs? What role does gender play in informal activities?
3. Student/adult relationships. What attitudes and actions do the students exhibit that express emulation (modeling) of adults or resistance to adults in the school or community? How do teachers express their attitudes concerning students through voice, actions, or programs? How do teachers exert authority or control? Does a teacher instill fear in children or is the teacher afraid of kids?
4. Health. What are the health conditions of students and teachers? What indications are there of how media, food, drink, drugs, tobacco, sleep (or lack of it), dress, makeup, and so forth are involved in lives of students and teachers?

5. Language and speech. How do language differences (including accents) among students and teachers affect academic work, informal relationships, tracking and other curricular programs?
6. Engagement with academics. How do students express their involvement and interest concerning the curriculum? How is competence expressed and recognized? How are gender differences seen in academic settings? How is lack of engagement expressed by students and dealt with by teachers? How are children responding to the curriculum? What is the curriculum?
7. Classroom culture. How do students organize and shape classroom activities? How is collective response or resistance shown? In what groups? Who plays what roles in the process? How do teachers attempt to influence group behavior?
8. School climate. What qualities are shown by the school as a whole? How does the building feel to you, physically, socially, and emotionally? Who seems to play a role in setting the social tone? What might result from the school climate in student behavior or achievement?

The arrangement asked for two forms of collaboration: (1) students would research a common topic at several schools and then analyze the differences; and (2) students using one school would analyze all the research topics, enabling them to see the school from multiple perspectives. Students met twice a week during on-campus class time, once with their common research topic group and once with their common school group. In both instances they were to bring their notes from their fieldwork and share their findings. Only the group that shared a common research topic made written reports. These reports, written by a different group member each week with credit given to individuals contributing to that week's work, reflected the insights gained from the different school visits as well as individual study of related research. The process was iterative: as the students acquired more information on the topic, they developed more critical observation and inquiry. The students educated each other in both these small group sessions as well as in larger lecture/discussion situations.

As mentioned earlier, in addition to the research topics, the students also interviewed teachers. The following questions were suggested for such conversations:

1. How long have you been a teacher?
2. Why did you decide on teaching as a career?
3. Are you credentialed? If so, what type?
4. Where did you receive your training?
5. How well prepared do you perceive yourself to be as a teacher of linguistically and culturally diverse children from low-income families?
6. How could you have been better prepared?
7. How much do you know about the lives of the children you teach? How have you been able to find out?
8. Have you ever done home visits?

These questions allowed teachers an opportunity to have a serious discussion with another informed adult who was interested in both their professional life and their relationship with students. They also were speaking with someone who had seen them teach and knew their students as well as the community from which the students came. Such situations were rare for teachers who tended to remain isolated within their classrooms or whose main venue for discussion is was the staff lunch room (for a sample of work with teachers, see Goodson & Walker, 1991).

REFLECTIONS ON TEACHING THE COURSE

I wanted my students to have the opportunity to link theory with practice while assisting in urban classrooms, but I had not yet become familiar with the procedures and politics of the school districts within commuting distance. I was sharing my plight with another faculty member from a more urban university who had previously been involved in one of the districts; she introduced me to the former assistant superintendent. As a result I was able to make further contacts with the administration of this particular district who welcomed my plan, providing me with access to all of its schools. It took about a month to get the initial placements sorted out after meeting with several principals and teachers. Fortunately, the public school's fall quarter session began in August, six weeks prior to the university's academic year.

Students who took the class came from all levels of academic preparation. Some were sophomores with no prior education courses, others were senior sociology majors who had had a great deal of theoretical material. Most students had been lulled into expecting lectures and exams. At first, students did not honor small group work or student presentations. They did not know how to take responsibility for sharing ideas in groups. After gaining confidence in my ability to orchestrate such a course in my new surroundings, with the commuter element intertwined, the students more quickly grasped the goals and procedures of the course. As I repeated the course, students who had taken the course previously asked if they could assist me in teaching it. These students served a pivotal role in the subsequent success of the course as they gave testimony to the transformative process of working with low-income, immigrant children.

The writing I assigned in the course was designed to progress from personal and informal to research-based and formal. The assignments included self-portraits, in-class "freewrites," group reports, a "synthesis" research paper, and take-home exams in the form of self-evaluations and evaluations of the field placement and group work. These evaluations included items such as:

1. Teachers: Would you recommend your teacher/s to future students in this course? Why or why not? How did she/he assist in your learning more about teaching?
2. Students: What events had the greatest impact on you?
3. Schools: How did principals or other teachers/staff contribute to or detract from your learning?

4. Overall:
   a. What did you learn from your experience?
   b. What were some turning points in your learning?
   c. Do you want to go into teaching more or less after this experience?
   d. Did it increase your commitment to teaching? If so, how?

STUDENT RESPONSES TO THE COURSE

The work of the students during the several offerings of the course was voluminous. The research papers truly synthesized the field work, research literature, and teacher interviews, as well as provided thoughtful responses to the course lectures and readings. A few comments from the final evaluations written by six students follow.

Sasha, a Filipino American female:

> I truly enjoyed going to the city and working with children at X Elementary. I told them I was Filipino and the Filipino kids became interested in me, came closer to me and started to ask me questions and speak Tagalog. From going to X Elementary and working with children, it encourages me to pursue the study of education with an emphasis on minority children.

Kathy, a Japanese American (san-sei) female:

> Working in a classroom at an urban school in the city was a wonderful experience for me. It is unlike any educational experience I have ever had before. The classroom makeup consisted of students of predominantly low-income families from diverse ethnic backgrounds and a White middle-class, middle-aged teacher. I learned so much listening to the kids in the class I worked with.

Lauren, a White European American female:

> My visits to the X school during the quarter were more influential and more powerful than I ever anticipated. Over

the past two years I have been exposed to both positive and negative aspects of American public schools but never have I been able to participate in and observe the actual complexity of issues that exist within one single classroom. My respect for all teachers has skyrocketed because of the variety of issues that they are not only expected to deal with but are compelled to deal with day in and day out. Monique is a prime example of the student who I felt benefited from my presence. Of course, the extent to which she enriched my life probably can go without articulating. My research at X school can be connected to the research ideas on the use of dialect and accent within the classroom in many ways.

Thomas, an African American male:

The observations I made enforced the ideas I gained from the readings and from my own research. Perhaps the most important thing about minority education that stood out from my observation was the need for teachers to spend time with each individual student in order to become knowledgeable about their students' lives and the problems they face in school. My experience with two students illuminated the notion of what language deficiency means for many kids. In the time I spent with them I was able to make them both feel confident of their multiplication and division skills as well as catch them up with what the rest of the class was learning about fractions. The teacher seemed really surprised at how much was accomplished. By the same token, I was really surprised at how quickly it took me to teach them the equivalent of an entire week's worth of math!

Myrian, a first generation Mexican American (Oaxacan) female:

Finally, what was not shown in the readings as much as I would like were the rewards of teaching, the love and respect that the students showed to me. The fieldwork was my only means of feeling this. I wish there would be some written articles about experiences like this one.

Shamryn, an Irish American female:

After going to my placement at X elementary school, I came to realize that our fieldwork was designed to be more of an eye-opener, a wake-up call if you will, telling us how it really is out there. This was a raw representation of what is truly going on in the public schools of our inner cities. I think having a placement such as this lets students, like myself, examine our motivations behind becoming a teacher and forced us to seriously think about whether or not we are cut out for such a demanding position. For some, the experience may have helped them to realize that teaching may not be the best way to use their talents and interests in education, and for others, it provided more insight and motivation to get out there into the schools and communities and make positive changes and contributions. The reading in this course proved to be just as empowering as the field placement because it often mirrored and helped me to make sense of what I was observing in the schools. I had the opportunity to see the marginalization, socialization, and assimilation that the course outlined first-hand, and I also saw the kids in the classrooms struggling with multiple identities as they struggled to rise above the disadvantaged label that was applied to them. I took this course because I don't feel I know enough about the experiences of minorities in our public education system; while my knowledge has grown immensely throughout the quarter, I still feel I need to learn and experience more before I'll be prepared to deal with what the teaching profession has in store for me. This course has provided me with some incredible insights from fellow classmates and I can't even begin to express the importance and the value of learning from my peers throughout the quarter. My research project has also opened many doors for me and has deepened my understanding of the importance of quality bilingual instruction immensely. I will continue to research this topic throughout my studies and hopefully one day I will be in a classroom like the one at X, contributing something positive to the lives of my students as well as continuing to learn from them, because students are the best teachers of all.

Perhaps the greatest compliment that came from this class was a student's asking if he or she could return to the district the following quarter, or sometimes for the entire year, to continue working in "my school" with "my kids." I have had numerous students do this. Some of them contracted with me for independent study, which meant that they had to turn in weekly field notes and essays on topics we had decided were of mutual concern. Often these topics arose during our conversations, which took place regularly as I heard their stories and guided their inquiry. Other students opted to volunteer without credit, keeping me informed without the requirements of paperwork. In addition, I also had students who, after taking this class with me and completing the education minor, asked me to find employment for them in the district. For example, one of my former students, an African American male (married to a Latina) contacted me from a youth camp where he and his wife were working and asked for assistance in finding them teaching jobs back at their "old school" where they had tutored two years before. I was able to help them find positions in one of the schools in the district.

CHAPTER 4

"Masks of Normality": Teacher Training on a Military Base

THIS CHAPTER IS ABOUT TRANSFORMATION AND DISCOURSE AND ABOUT shedding preconceived ideas in order to assist in the healing and growth of adults who have far more in common with 70 percent of our K–12 population than do our mainstream teacher-education students. It is also about a group of individuals who initially I would have contended should never be prepared for the teaching force. It is about respect for differences in areas seldom discussed. In working with a group of "mature" students who met my own stereotypes of normality, I learned about the importance of self-portraiture and disclosure among students. I also came to appreciate the value of a critique of education based on understanding life's larger realities. This process I call "masks of normality."

I was asked to teach a course about the political and economic context of American schooling to twenty-four individuals at a naval base on a remote island tucked amidst the beauty of the American Northwest. I was very reluctant to accept the assignment even though I had taught the course previously on our university campus; I just did not want to work with this particular population. I did not want to be the first faculty member from our university to prepare retiring military personnel and their spouses for the teaching profession. The course was to be offered in a small conservative town, just off the base. It would take me almost two hours to get there on a winding country road, a four-hour evening class during winter, which meant dealing with rain and snow in the dark. I did not want to do this. These were my ostensible reservations. My real concern was my own latent prejudice against the military. My brother had died of spinal meningitis while in boot camp. Born in England, having traversed through Asia, he was a gentle soul offered up for sacrifice to a country he little understood and had less interest in defending. Layering this pain was my own critical analysis of the military-industrial complex and how it has raped our country of human and material resources. No, I did not want to go, but I did.

During the first meeting of class I realized that most of the students were associated with conservative Christian churches as well as with the military. Having been raised by a Scots-Irish father and an English mother in a minefield of fundamentalist religion that differentiated between "the chosen," my father, and "the lost," my mother, I breathed deeply as I gazed into the White faces of what I considered the worst of "middle America." I was baffled as to how I would move these apparently rigid and dogmatic military minds toward understanding how a so-called democracy continues to produce unequal educational opportunities for its citizens. I began with the assumption that educating military people for the teaching force was a misguided adventure. I judged these individuals based on the color of their skin and their profession, assuming that the latter was an indication of their political and educational beliefs. The ramifications of such thinking when generalized to other groups were obvious. I was an urban educator familiar with communities of color, diversity, and inner cities. While I taught and preached moving beyond assumptions of skin color, accent, language, dress, and class, I cringed at the prospect of working for ten long weeks with a group of White people with whom I presumed I had little in common.

I was determined not to dilute my readings. This was a course in the social foundations of education. They would learn, as my other students had, what has differentiated the schooled from the illiterate. They would come to understand power politics, racism, ignorance, and the universal desire of all peoples to see their children survive and succeed. My readings included essays by Larry Cuban, John Goodlad, James Comer, Elliot Eisner, and Albert Shanker (in Burleson, 1991); *Deschooling Society*, by Ivan Illich (1970); *Pedagogy of the Oppressed,* by Paulo Freire (1970); *The Persistent Problems of Education*, by Paul Woodring (1983); "Class, Race, and Gender in Educational Politics," in *Postmodern Education* by Aronowitz and Giroux (1991); "Education" in Lee Maracle's *I Am Woman* (1988); *Lives on the Boundary*, by Mike Rose (1988); *Savage Inequalities*, by Jonathan Kozol (1991); and "How It Happened: The Legal Status of Women and People of Color in the United States" in Paula Rothenberg's *Race, Class, and Gender in the United States* (1992).

I entered what I perceived to be a den of lions, only to awaken ten days later—after having read their self-portraits—to individuals with real needs, pain, and a desire to work with children from all walks of life. What I had forgotten is that many of the people who join the military do so out of frustration with life and think that they have nowhere else to go. Many are from working-class backgrounds who did not do well in school. For some it is the choice between welfare and/or low-paying, unskilled jobs, or technical training in the military. For others it is not a choice. Their parents, whether out of patriotism, fear of inner-city streets, or rural poverty, demanded that their children enter the service. I am not talking about Rambos. I am talking about individuals who convinced themselves, or were convinced, that the military was their way "out."

The class of twenty-six students was about half male, half female; average age was around thirty-five, ranging from twenty-two to fifty-two years of age, including a mother-daughter combination. The group came across as strong and determined and willing to challenge my authority. The women were connected to the military as wives, children, or navy personnel themselves. More than half of the men were on the verge of retiring from the military at around forty years of age. They had another twenty years of productive employment in front of them, and they wanted to become teachers. The stereotypes that each sex had of the other, as well as about inner-city children, people of color, and welfare recipients were clear from the start. Gradually, I moved forward with detached curiosity at what I had engaged.

SELF-PORTRAITS

One technique I have used with all my students regardless of the course content, and which I, in turn, have encouraged them to use with their students, is the writing of self-portraits. For nontraditional students, this is imperative. One cannot, and should not, assume one knows the individual behind the mask of facial features that we so readily stereotype. The purpose of the portrait is not only for me to know the students' backgrounds but for me gingerly to use the information to fill in gaps and address issues. The writing also requires them to reflect on their own experiences with schooling and the implications thereof for their philosophy of education.

But with this class an additional hidden agenda arose, particularly from the women. In their self-portraits and weekly writings they expressed thanks not only for being asked to speak honestly on paper but also for having entrusted the information to someone who they felt would in some way use their stories to educate those in the class who symbolized "the oppressor," either husband, boyfriend, or father. These women who appeared superficially to be middle-class, well grounded, and on the road to heaven, had in fact lived shattered lives because of excessive military transfers, inadequate education, disciplinarian fathers, and/or abusive husbands. Their self-portraits were filled with hatred, anger, insecurity, and fear. Some had dropped out of school due to pregnancy and/or rebellion. Most had been poor. Some were single mothers and/or had been on welfare. They were overwhelmed at the thought of returning to school. For about one-third of the women this was their first try back at college after twenty years. Sitting in the same room with people who had their B.A.'s and careers as military officers compounded their insecurity. Mira wrote in her self-portrait: "I was born in Oklahoma, on a naval base. My family moved twelve times before I was sixteen. In nine years of schooling I attended twelve schools, then dropped out while in the tenth grade. After my marriage at age sixteen. . . . " She later continued, "While working in a factory and cleaning houses, I learned a lot about how people can be mistreated and the meaning of 'sweat shop.' I decided I needed my GED and would go to college. I wanted out of poverty!" She concluded, "My great fear is that I will fail to do well. Some feelings of inadequacy are hard to overcome."

Having heard calls from some of the men for sterilization of teenage mothers, a "return to basics," and for Christian family values, I knew that they did not know the women who sat beside them. But as time elapsed, the ignorance of the women became equally apparent. The images that these women had of "their men" proved unfounded. Ironically, as the portraits revealed, the men in fact did not fare much better in self-esteem. While most came across as confident, loud, conservative, and educated, their writing etched a radically different profile. Their bravado proved to be a screen for their working-class roots, their lack of adequate education, and their dubious self-images. Due to the constant movement of navy assignments, many had disconnected schooling and dysfunctional families. Some had been "special ed. cases" themselves. It was as if the writing served as a purging, a conduit stopped up for years due to the demands of "manhood" in the military. Secret realities of lives unseen in this sea of White people and unspoken in this naval community flowed across the pages. John wrote:

> I lost my scholarship at the end of my junior year of college. My parents were disappointed but did not berate me. They never attended college. My father has only a GED although he made a good living in the construction industry. Just last year my mother finally obtained her high school diploma. Looking for a job, I came to the startling realization that 3 years of college was tantamount to no college. I finally was hired by the State of Kentucky as a prison guard. After 2 years, I realized this career would take me nowhere; I enlisted in the Navy. Because of my previous experience with the psychiatric unit at the prison, I was selected as a drug abuse counselor.

The question before me each week was how to work with this group, how to bring up issues in a way that would empower the group, both women and men, to trust each other enough to open up and take responsibility for their unique lives and, hence, perceptions. Would they assist me in the educational process? The first two weeks were rough for us all. Could we keep this ship afloat long enough to figure out where we were going? We did. In the remaining part of this chapter, I will explore some the methods used to convey their stories in a respectful manner and their desire for me to act as midwife in delivering their identity and pain to the larger class.

Introductions during the first class session included a recounting of my own struggles with education and why I do what I do as a profession. I explained one reason for sharing this personal story was because I would not ask them to do what I would not do myself and their first assignment for me was to write a self-portrait. Trust was important. Next, I had them relate their perception of the "most persistent problem" in education. This was the first time that I heard their voices and they spoke with some conviction. I responded to each "problem" and inquired further into their definitions and their reasons, and alluded to research in the area. Having heard these ideas, we then discussed possible topics that they might want to explore for a final paper and presentation. The topics were to relate to their concerns, to something that they had been wanting to find out about. Finally, we discussed the reading assignments, and how they, the students, would take responsibility for the presentation of the chapters each week; they were to work in pairs and meet outside of class. They could "teach" the content of the readings to the class in any way they found suitable. I assigned them to write a self-portrait based on questions I had handed out and to write down their topic and define the terms.

Ironically, although the students felt more vulnerable after having written self-portraits, they felt empowered at the same time. They responded to me differently, as if I had knowledge of their real selves. Some asked if I would keep their work confidential; and others asked if they could share it with the class; some apologized for writing so much; and others thanked me for the opportunity to review their education and to consider how it had impacted their decision to become a teacher. They signed up in pairs for weekly presentations of the readings. Each person was to present twice during the quarter. In addition to the weekly readings, all students had to write down and turn in three questions, concerns, or points of clarification for each chapter. I used this as an accountability factor to check that they were indeed doing the reading, which was the basis for discussion. If they wrote ideas down as they read, they came to class with notes to review. The weekly writing also provided me with another avenue through which to encourage their individual voices. Similarly, it gave them the opportunity to dialogue with me about ideas and issues that came up in class but about which they were hesitant to speak.

By the third week I had read all their self-portraits and knew what was behind some of their reasoning for selecting their particular topic and "persistent problem in education." I grouped them according to similar topics, knowing that many of them were using the same language to mean very different things, such as "back to basics," "more discipline," "family values." They met in groups outside class and came up with a joint final presentation, discussing how the readings did or did not illuminate their points of view on the topic. I knew that part of the educational process had to come from within the group. They had to become real, which meant they had to become vulnerable.

We began the class session with presentations on the readings. There was bravado on the males' side, with some important exceptions, and retreat by women who shunned confrontation or conflict. I knew I had to dispel numerous stereotypes, particularly as they apply to people of color, urban schools, and immigrants. I felt the need to unmask the self-righteousness that assumed that those in the room were beyond "reproach." This was a delicate process: how could I empower them while at the same time taking them down a notch? how much trust had we established?

As if on cue, the transformation started to occur. I knew that I knew more about their lives than they knew of each other's. I knew about their family's educational level, socioeconomic status, region of birth, schooling patterns, and so forth. More important was the fact that they knew that I knew. The readings had provoked accusations and generalizations; their writings on the assigned topics provided them an opportunity to demonstrate strength of conviction. In private, written comments, I responded to and challenged some of their basic beliefs while validating their inquiry. As self-disclosure in essays moved into open discussion, we all came to know that one person had adopted two children with AIDS, another had a son in prison, two others had adopted children of color, and several had not made it through high school.

In the middle of a heated debate, the assumption emerged that welfare recipients and dropouts were mainly people of color and that teen pregnancy was a new and growing phenomenon. I looked over to Pat, a high school drop-out and abused woman of forty. She knew about welfare. She also blamed home schooling and the "back to basics" movement for her twenty-year-old son's fourth-grade reading level. She said, "I dropped out of high school at the beginning of my sophomore year. I wanted to get an education but both my parents had been drop-outs and it just seemed natural to follow in their footsteps. I married and got a job in a factory when I was eighteen years old."

Before Pat finished her story, someone raised her hand. Susan wanted people to know that it was not just the poor who go on welfare. From a middle-class family, she was forced to join the ranks of unemployment when her fiancé left her with child. Susan recalled, "College was hard won and very eye-opening. I went through on scholarships and welfare, raising my illegitimate son with no other assistance. We lived in very bad areas and I saw what could happen to us if I did not keep going. Out of college, I joined the navy for job security to support my son. As a single mom for twelve years, money and security were important." What she did not reveal at the time was that her son's father was Mexican. Having heard the racist remarks in class she was hesitant to expose this fact. Two weeks and many honest conversations later, she brought her son to class to sit and listen and observe.

As the weeks progressed, more stories, more counter-views, and more real people evolved as the truths of working-class life gained dominance over the lies of military compliance. One of the most powerful evenings was when one of the youngest, most well-schooled, and most proper-looking students haltingly told us that her sister was a prostitute. While not a prostitute herself, this student's knowledge of the sex industry, its patrons and pimps, was shocking. Those who had assumed this woman not only to be above them academically but also removed from them psychologically, readjusted their assumptions and granted her new space for acceptance.

Near the end of the quarter at one session I had to leave this four-hour class halfway through in order to catch a flight for a national conference. I was reluctant to cancel the class, concerned about convening for only two hours, and hesitant to allow them to continue without my being present. What occurred demonstrated to me how far this group had come in terms of level of engagement and mutual respect. At the start of class they informed me that it truly was not necessary for me to stay; I could leave any time and they would handle the presentations and discussion themselves. Even while I remained present, they organized the format and announced the reading assignments for the following week. I sat back and watched; they glanced toward me and smiled, "Really it's OK, you can go. Drive carefully." I hesitated but agreed. The following week they stayed for five hours instead of four recounting who debated which viewpoint, all the while assuring me that even though the discussion was intense, it was never explosive. In fact, it was one of the best nights they had had as a group, just a group sitting around talking about issues that they had come to see as imperative to their understanding not only of education and teaching but also of life.

What had happened in these ten weeks? Two examples from their writing might best reflect the transformations that had taken place. The following are from their responses to Mike Rose's *Lives On the Boundary* (1988). Pat wrote:

John Dewey recognized long ago that "only in education, never in the life of the farmer, sailor, merchant, physician, or laboratory experimenter, does knowledge mean a store of information aloof from doing." Often people of low socioeconomic status have not been exposed to the scholarly language of the elite. This does not mean that they are less intelligent, it just means they need more exposure to the language. They need to have plenty of opportunities to discuss and write about what they are learning—they need to be challenged to think critically about what they are learning, and apply this knowledge to solve problems.

This book has been an encouragement to me. I was pretty sure that I would have to drop out of this program. I was intimidated by the educational backgrounds of my classmates; I felt very inadequate. I enjoyed the readings and discussion, but I felt I had very little to offer. I now recognize that many students experience these feelings, and the only way to succeed is to stick with the program. Even if I am not an "A" student, I will learn something. I also know that if I quit; my children may follow my example.

Mitch wrote,

Among the many new people I met on the pages of Rose's book, I encountered an old familiar character—me. Since I've achieved a modicum of academic and professional success, I never considered myself to be "educationally under prepared." However, my preconceived notions of who constituted the "educationally under prepared" (immigrants, minorities, poor, the handicapped) were shattered as I marveled at the similarities between my background and that of the author. Like Rose, I was raised by undereducated, working-class parents in an uninspiring urban environment. I too attended Catholic schools and a small Jesuit liberal arts college, "doing what I had to do to get by, and with half a mind." Unlike Rose, unfortunately, a cavalry of mentors never rode to my academic rescue. Halfway through my normal life expectancy, the legacy of my educational experience is moderate success, a lack of self-confidence, and a gnawing feeling that I am more capable than the academic skills I've attained allow me to express. In the military, I found the "passion about a cause or idea" (patriotism) which Rose believes is so essential to success. However, this passion has been tempered by the realization that only a quality education separates me and many of my shipmates from the politicians who commit our lives to misadventures throughout the world. The volunteer military is comprised of the sons and daughters of middle and working-class America—there are few Harvard, Stanford, or Yale Law School graduates in the ranks. Mike Rose's passion and commitment stirred the embers of idealism and optimism that had once burned brightly within me but which had grown dim with time and experience. Why continue to follow my instincts, to aspire to be the kind of teacher who can make a difference, to do my part to make my community and country better for everyone? Simply because it's the right thing to do.

So, how can we move beyond the masks, including our own? The academic and professional setting of college life reinforces the perception of the need for masks to protect us from assumptions, questions, and, hence, pain. The temptation is great to hide our working-class roots and the gaps in our education. We hope no one will inquire too closely about the "missing years" on our résumé. We walk on eggs fearing we will be "found out." This is no way to construct a life. I tell my students, as I have come to believe myself, that struggles are transformative experiences. They are gifts to be shared, not hoarded or hidden. They are bridges that enable us to link with others, our students and colleagues, on more meaningful levels than our professional roles permit. To do otherwise is to deny a part of ourselves that is necessary, not only for our success, but for our survival. The mask of normality is dangerous and destructive in that it perpetuates the mythology that only certain people are allowed into and successful in academia; it creates the illusion of conformity where it does not exist.

CHAPTER 5

Confronting the Larger Community of Helping Professionals

LIKE MANY MAJOR RESEARCH UNIVERSITIES, MY HOME CAMPUS HAD ONLY meager success in reaching into working-class communities to serve the unique needs of individuals who were not able to commute to the flagship institution because of family or employment obligations. To mitigate this weakness, my university followed suit and established branch campuses. I was invited to join such an effort along with several others who had a background in working with students from diverse linguistic and cultural backgrounds. Our assignment was to establish a teacher education program that would be responsive to the needs of the local community. The goal of the program was to increase the number of teachers who could work effectively with urban, low-income students. The subtext was to increase the number of teachers of color.

Even though the mission of the branch campus advocated service to the community, the inherently elitist decision making within higher education opted to offer only upper division coursework, thus barring many local applicants from participating in the programs. Given that the campus was located in a working-class city where the link for many students into higher education was through community college, it would have been logical to have at least attempted to bridge the two, often separate, levels by offering some programs that spanned the needs of four-year students. The branch campus, envisioned as a conduit for strong community college graduates to continue their education, lacked the means to reach effectively the students within its immediate area. As a result, most of the students who came into our program were not working-class and even fewer were students of color.

Students in the local K–12 schools were not faring well. Many teachers were unaware of the needs of their students and even less inclined to find out. Fear and ignorance pervaded many schools. The likelihood that many students from these schools would be able to move through high school and survive four years of higher education and then enter a graduate program in teaching was slim. Nevertheless, the need for teachers from the community who could relate to the children in front of them was great. The superintendent of the school district, an African American male held in great esteem by many, was so committed to this goal that he found time to teach a course for pre-service teachers in our program. Still, we had only two African American students in a sea of whiteness with a sprinkling of single representatives from other ethnicities. This lack of ethnic diversity would not have bothered me so much had there been a wider range of experience and insights among the White students from which to draw. I do not hold to the assumption that one's visual identity guarantees one's understanding of all people who have a similar visage. I have seen too many examples to the contrary. But whether such is the case or not, it is incumbent upon us to address the needs of the children who are with us now; we cannot wait until there are enough teachers whose background matches those of urban youth to begin this effort.

Realizing the precarious nature of a program intended to prepare teachers for urban multicultural classrooms when so little diversity of experience existed among the students themselves, I designed a course, titled "Multicultural Education: Critical Issues," to give pre-service teachers a sense of the larger community in which their students operated. The course was to provide a critical exploration of the major intellectual, political, and pedagogical issues in multicultural education. We considered the leading proponents and critics of multicultural education, studied institutional and cultural discrimination (related to race and ethnicity, class, and gender), and explored the relationship between schooling and the reproduction of stratification and discrimination. The required texts were *Freedom's Plow* (Perry & Fraser, 1993), plus a wide array of topical readings in *Change/Education: Issues in Perspective* (Smith, 1993). In addition to the usual combination of self-portrait, discussion of readings with student leadership, and an essay on educational reform, the major work of the course required community involvement in the form of visits to local social service agencies that impact youth and their families.

My goal was not only to introduce future teachers to the other institutions that respond to the needs of children and their families but also to provide them with a reality check on what it means to be required to function within the constraints of some of these social service agencies in order to survive. In addition, I wanted them to understand how attitudes toward institutions, authority figures, education, and teachers might be formed based on their families' experiences. Throughout the quarter students shared their community encounters in a variety of formats, including field notes, essays, class presentations, and a final synthesis paper.

The campus was in a highly diverse, working-class community that spent the late 1970s and 1980s in a economic slump only to recover in the late 1990s. The city embraced the establishment of a new branch campus as part of urban renewal and revitalization. The strategic placement required extensive negotiations with the community as well as a commitment to serve the needs of the current population, which included the African American community with significant historical roots in the city. Although largely working-class and White, the community increasingly included Latinos, Southeast Asians, and Eastern Europeans as prospects of employment improved in the city.

To make the exercise meaningful, the selection of social service agencies had to reflect those in highest demand by the children in this area. From my own research and knowledge of the city, I came up with a list that was broad enough for every student to be able to choose at least one with which he or she felt comfortable. Possibilities included a homeless shelter, food bank, juvenile court, detention centers, YMCA after-school programs, family centers, Salvation Army, Big Brother/Sister, rehabilitation programs, a shelter for battered women, ethnic churches, and literacy centers.

I suggested that if they had time, the students could volunteer for a few hours over the course of the quarter. In addition to the observations of the people who worked in the agencies as well as the clients, students were expected to engage in both casual and more formal conversations with the people in at least three agencies. I stated a preference that they go alone as I wanted them to gain a sense of hesitancy, discomfort, and isolation that many who have had to be "serviced" feel. After several hours within one agency, students were to come away and summarize their encounters, reflecting on and responding to several questions, such as: How do you think you were perceived by the clients in the institution or program you visited? How did you feel going through the process? What did you learn about yourself? Others? How has this experience altered the way you view education and youth? How will this knowledge transform the way you work with your students?

The story of Connie demonstrates how the process evolved for my students. A single mother of a six year old who had been identified by teachers as "developmentally delayed," Connie had been criticized for not doing enough to help her child. She herself had been abused by the system, criticized by teachers, and labeled a "bad mother." She was now back in school after several aborted attempts to complete a B.A. and was committed to becoming a teacher. To prepare for her journey into the world of social service agencies, Connie opted to interview three people in her own community who might give her insights into how they worked with low-income parents. One of these people was her own child's teacher, who had not only taught in an urban, low-income community in Harlem in New York City but had conducted home visits with all of her students her first year there. She then spoke with a special education counselor who shared with her the complexity of the advising system as well as stories of children who "get lost in the paper work." Lastly, she visited the principal of one of the most racially diverse elementary schools in the area who informed her that he had mandated that all

teachers would hold pre-conferences in the students' homes before the first day of school.

Having this knowledge and experience, she felt equipped to
begin her inquiry into the children's experience in the wider
community. Stopping by the local Boys and Girls Club to see if
she could connect with some parents, she happened to get an ap-
pointment with one of the program directors. The director was
delighted that a prospective teacher was proactively trying to
gain an understanding of the complexity of students' and parents' lives. A couple of the children took Connie on a tour of the
facility, sharing their stories along the way. Connie asked the director for help in connecting with some of the parents of the children. The director agreed to do so and promised to get back to
her. After a week and no reply, Connie, to her credit, went back
to the club to inquire about the progress of the contacts. The director, claiming heavy workload, guaranteed her that within a
week she would come up with names of parents whom Connie
could contact. She did.

In the meantime, Connie struck out into other parts of the
community, visiting the local food bank that provided government surplus food to the needy. One of the workers suggested
that she visit the Martin Luther King Shelter and gave her a
contact, Justina. Justina invited her to the next parent meeting,
knowing that since attendance was mandatory in order to stay
at the shelter, everyone would be there. By chance, the other
person who had been scheduled to speak at the shelter that
evening canceled, and Connie was able to use the entire meeting
to talk to the parents about their children. Some of the parents
in the shelter had up to six children with them, ranging in age
from one to twelve. About half of the residents were African
American and the other half, White European. Not all of the residents were women, about one third were men. Most were single
but one couple was married. Connie's success in gaining access
to this group's thoughts and concerns had partially to do with
her own willingness to share the fact that she had a daughter
with fairly severe special needs, which Connie felt incapable of
responding to in a way that could truly help her in school. Teachers would send home "reams of paper instructing me on how to

work with my child, but I was too intimidated to ask for help." She talked of how blame is transferred to parents when their children are not perceived as "normal" or "well behaved." She told them that before she became a teacher, she needed to know more about what promotes positive relationships with parents, particularly those who may be under stress. After her disclosures, the several parents told of the circumstances that brought them to the shelter and how, through it all, education remained a priority for their children.

Meanwhile, the Boys and Girls Club director set up appointments with four parents for Connie. In each case, the importance of teachers communicating with parents took precedence over the personal trials of the family. Finally, Connie talked to a parent coordinator at one of the alternative schools in a predominantly African American part of town. She wanted to know what made teachers build walls between themselves and parents. The response was one she had heard in our class repeatedly but, after conducting her own interviews with a range of experts in the field, found to ring even more true: fear. "Teachers are afraid of being questioned by parents and having their authority undermined."

Most of the teacher education students came away with a new appreciation for the complexity of the lives of their students and their families. Several students were dumbfounded by the red tape that people had to confront in order to receive assistance. Some of them waited for hours at the site to see how long it took actually to get processed, talking to people about their attitudes toward education and the larger issues that detract from a child's success in school. Repeatedly, the students heard stories of the child who was required to stay home with younger children or an ailing relative in order for the parent, usually the mother, to attend to one of these institutional demands. Previously, the students perceived the children and their families as being irresponsible, uncaring. After these interviews, the picture altered radically, as one teacher education student said: "I no longer see students as irresponsible; in reality, they are super-responsible. They, as children, have to contend with matters that I never even knew existed. They are taking on the burdens most adults would bend under."

A common assumption among educators holds that the absenteeism and apparent irresponsibility demonstrated by low-income students in classrooms around the country is largely because of the attitude of both students and parents toward education. While this does have some validity, far more often students are absent from classrooms or delinquent with homework because of outside demands on their lives, demands unseen and uninterrogated in most public school settings.

CHAPTER 6

Home Visits

WHILE A COMPANY WOULD NOT CONSIDER ESTABLISHING A BUSINESS OR selling a product without intense study of the region, the customers, and the demand for the product, most educators enter schools ill informed, if not ignorant, of the children they are about to teach and the community from which they come (Jehl and Kirst, 1992). This disjunction is most frequently attributed to middle-class teachers who work with low-income urban youth. Yet, in my teaching of widely diverse graduate students who are teachers, principals, and health professionals, I have found their lack of knowledge of students' lives profound. In this chapter I look at the outcomes and processes of home visits. While the phenomenon of sending teachers into the homes of their students is not new, it is a rare occurrence in inner-city schools today. There are a variety of reasons for the reluctance of teachers to do home visits, most of them cloaked in assumptions around lack of time, limitations on the rights of teachers, and, in a candid moment, fear of entering into the lives of their students.

Traditionally, teachers have taught in their neighborhood school (Sarason, 1982). This provided children and teachers with the opportunity to see each other in a variety of nonacademic situations such as the grocery store, the local church, or on the street. This was even true in urban schools, especially prior to desegregation and the popularization of the automobile. With desegregation came middle-class movement out of urban areas to the suburbs. With cars came the option for teachers to commute to work. Soon teachers of inner-city kids, regardless of their ethnicity, were opting to live in middle-class neighborhoods removed from the poverty and congestion of urban life. Teachers no longer knew the families of their children; they did not ride on the same buses; they did not shop in the same stores. With separation came increased assumptions of how the other "half" lived. Having little to refute the stories of urban decline or an understanding of how middle-class flight contributed to the plight of those left behind, teachers became more and more estranged from their students.

While my own research and that of others have demonstrated that teachers whose life experiences more closely approximate the lives of the children they teach are often more aware of the needs of their students, we cannot draw a simplistic conclusion that children learn best from those who look most like them. There is too much evidence to contradict the assumption that simply because one is of a particular ethnicity, one has the ability to teach the children of one's community or culture. In fact, if we are talking about working with low-income children, there is evidence that shows that teachers who have come from working-class backgrounds may be less inclined to work with low-income children. There are a number of factors for this "distancing," including the recent acquisition of middle-class status and the desire to work in an environment (school/community) that demonstrates one's upward movement in social status; fear of being reidentified with a group from which one has emerged; and the pain of working with students who may be similar to the ones that ostracized or penalized one for being more academic as a child.

The importance of connecting teachers with the community in which they teach and more specifically with the families of their students is often ignored in the literature on educational reform that stresses to diversity. If parental/guardian involvement is discussed, it is often in the context of how to bring "them" into the school (Epstein, 1986). Complaints abound over the low participation of low-income parents in schools, including not volunteering, not attending P.T.S.A. meetings, not showing up for "back to school nights," and so forth. The reasons for low parental participation in school life by working-class and low-income families have been discussed extensively in the literature. One reason is the perception by most working-class individuals that teachers are the professionals responsible for the education of their children, not parents. Parents will profess to teach their children morals, religion, language, discipline, and respect, but they expect teachers to teach their children the academic basics. Many parents are confused as to why teachers are upset when they do not help a child with schoolwork and perplexed why a child might be perceived as less capable because the parents are not educated. I have often heard it said: "Isn't it up to the teacher to do the teaching? What has this got to do with parents? I have my job, why don't they do theirs? Why do they expect me to come in and do their job for them too?" Working-class parents who have not received much education, particularly in this country, or who have had negative experiences with education also hesitate to enter schools because they feel they are not worthy, that they will be misunderstood, or that they will embarrass their child. I have known parents who did not think that they had the appropriate clothes to wear to go to the school or who felt that their accent might be misinterpreted as ignorance or that they might be asked a question that they could not answer. My own parents felt all of these things.

This does not mean that parents lack an interest in their child's education nor that they fail to attempt to provide a context in which children can have some time and space to study at home. The reality is that many working-class parents do not have the frame of reference for the demands of American schooling. My parents always thought that homework was a sign of my inability to finish my work at school. Reading at home was not acceptable as my mother thought that children should be outside playing physically and not "under foot." Homework was done on the kitchen table after dinner with everyone else buzzing about. Mom helped color in my maps; that is all she could do as she left school at age thirteen for work in a factory. The situation is not the same for most middle-class and upper-middle-class families. These parents often perceive they have the right to, and responsibility for, directing the course of their child's education. They volunteer for school activities, tutor in classrooms, talk to the administration and counselors about the establishment of more and better programs, and advocate for special attention to their child's needs. They are often, ironically, the nemesis of new teachers. Seldom do they respect teachers as professionals in the same way as working-class parents.

"Parent conferences" are one of the few times that most parents enter schools to talk with teachers. These meetings, however, are often a quick thirty-minute talk to parents by three to five other "educational experts" about their child who is seldom present. The situation, to say the least, can be disempowering for parents or guardians as they hear about their child's behavior and academic abilities, which are usually not up to snuff. The power differential is exacerbated by the technical language used by educators that they themselves often resent but by which they are bound. Parents are left in a haze as they hear things about their child that they have never seen. The context of school measures and defines attributes and skills that often are not asked for within the home. A mother who sees her child as reliable, responsible, strong, and nurturing as he cares for his siblings and works to assist the family is told by professionals that he is lazy, lagging behind his peers academically, and cannot proceed to the next grade level. Names of tests, SAT 9, PSAT, SAT, STAR, flash through the conversation like glimpses of the sun on a windy, cloud-filled day. Too embarrassed to ask for clarification or definition, parents, treated like children, leave filled with anger, muted by their own fear of appearing more ignorant than their child who has clearly already been condemned as such. The exercise of unequal power subjectifies the individual to the point of consenting to his or her own oppression.

In this chapter I argue for a way of reversing this power dynamic by placing the parent in the role of expert and the teacher in the position of learner in the form of home visits. Requiring home visits of many of my graduate students over the years in a variety of very different situations, I have seen only successes. Still, the resistance to home visits is exceedingly great. The reasons are valid and need to be addressed, but the benefits, once experienced, far outweigh the time required or the risks taken. The most common reasons given for not visiting the homes of the children we teach include: lack of time, irrelevance to teaching, a duty beyond the responsibility or role of a teacher, the perception that one might not be well received, and the fear of entering the homes of our students, particularly if they are from low-income families. While some say the fear is real and that many parents are unstable, I have never had a student teacher not welcomed in the home of a student. For many parents, it is a time to be celebrated. In all cases, my student teachers have been served food and beverage as the scenarios below will reveal. What is learned in an hour-long home visit can seldom be acquired within the confines of a school.

By bridging the gap between understanding urban students and a commitment to them, home visits and the resulting dialogue between teachers and family members can provide the critical shift in stereotypical attributions and other limitations in teachers' work with their students. By looking closely at a few specific home-visit dialogues, I hope to show the basis for the transformation reported by the student teachers and the resulting changes in attitude and performance of all concerned both within the schooling context and the home environment. I argue not only for the importance of home visits but for greater involvement in the lives of our students.

I will focus on three home-visit case studies conducted in two different classes of graduate students. The first, a study of Tami, was selected from a class of practicing teachers who returned to graduate school for their M.A. after having taught in public schools for some time. The other two case studies are of student teachers, Amelia and Marianna, who were in their second year of a M.A.T. (teacher certification) program. By the time of this assignment, Amelia and Marianna had spent significant time working with master teachers but had not taught a class solo. Excerpts from their interviews with parents and guardians as well as from their final summaries for the course demonstrate the transformative process that these teacher/students went through.

TAMI

While working with veteran teachers who were simultaneously enrolled in a master's program in a larger urban school district, I became aware that many of these individuals held hostile and dangerous assumptions about their students and the communities from whence the children came. As we went through the course readings, the students candidly revealed their prejudices and fears. When I suggested that some home visits might illuminate their understanding of the children in their care, they clearly resisted. The resistance was not unfounded.

One of the students, Tami, had never seen an African American face to face before moving to the state three years earlier at age twenty-five. She commented, "My views of Blacks have been totally shaped by the media and my husband." She was married to a policeman, her high school sweetheart, who patroled the "central district" at night and came home filled with stories of gangs, knifings, drugs, and danger. This was the district that Tami's first-graders called home. Initially, the prospect of my requiring that she conduct interviews with the parents of her students in this neighborhood was beyond her comprehension. I asked her to discuss it with her husband. He said she could not go. Ironically, his resistance was matched by her growing curiosity based on our discussions and the readings in class, which were opening up another world to her. There was, however, another factor that prompted her finally to agree to the home visits. She revealed to me that earlier in the year she had been called a "racist" by one of the parents at school. Tami asked the parent what she had done to deserve such an appellation. The parent said that Tami had treated her son in a discriminatory fashion. Demonstrating a fortitude that I was not sure existed, Tami told me, "I need to know what I did wrong."

In reality, school as an institution is a self-enclosed process in which teachers are in control. To move outside of this context is to open oneself to vulnerability. By the fifth week of my class Tami was ready and willing to make home visits (the other students had begun their interviews by week three). Tami asked for explicit instructions on everything: what to wear? what to say when she called up and asked to visit? how to resppond to a refusal to visit or to tape record? whether to have a companion for safety's sake? She made the calls; they welcomed her. To my amazement she had told them on the phone, forthrightly, that she had never been to an African American home and indeed had never talked to "one of them" outside of the classroom and did not know what to expect. They told her "Come on round. We have more reason to fear you than you do to fear us."

On her initial visit, she arrived, finding a single-family home with a well-kept lawn and little fence. It was in a rough neighborhood but not as bad as she had imagined. She was greeted by the student's mother, and to her amazement, his father. She had assumed that the child had come from a single-parent home. The house was immaculate. Later in class, she said, "They even had a VCR. I didn't think Black people had all the same stuff that we do in their homes." Finding myself embarrassed by her ignorance and fearing what she might have said to the parents of the child, I asked to listen to the tape recordings of the interview in addition to her edited transcription.

During the course of the interview I found out that Tami, who was pregnant at the time, ended up spending two hours with the family discussing everything from breast-feeding to slavery. She came to realize that she had a great deal in common with these parents; they had knowledge and advice she needed not just about their son, her student, but about Tami's future child. At one point the parents gave Tami a brief review of African American history in one of the most gentle and caring tones I have ever heard. They were taken by her ingenuousness and she by their willingness to accept her. The following week she asked if her husband could visit my class. He did. She told me, "I don't want my child to grow up thinking that black people are different from us. I never knew. Now I do."

TWO STUDENT TEACHERS

In a radically different world, a coastal farmworking community nested in green pungent fields of cabbage and artichokes, two home visits took place that portray a similar transformation. In both cases my students accompanied their master teachers to a home visit as a requirement for my course. My intention was that my student teachers have an opportunity not only to visit the home of at least one of the children in their class but also to see how the dynamics of teacher and parent shift when out of the classroom context. The two cases are quite different yet both provide insights about the children they were teaching and about the children's behavior within the schooling context. Both are powerful and painful. Both interviews were conducted in Spanish as the parents of the children did not speak English. Only one of the students, Amelia, spoke fluent Spanish; the two master teachers and the other student teacher, Marianna, while not native speakers, knew enough Spanish to communicate. Both stories are in the words of the student teacher.

Amelia

We finally pull up into a gravel driveway leading up to a buttercup yellow house. Roberto is expecting us on the porch. He waves at Kathy and me excitedly and disappears into the house. A petite smiling woman emerges. "Pasenle!'" she beckons. "What a beautiful home you have!" exclaims Kathy. "Gracias, it is at your disposal," she responds, her cheeks beginning to blush. The living room emits a welcoming warmth. My eyes dance over all the hand-made lace curtains and beautiful crochet table covers. A family portrait sits on the coffee table amongst some statues of saints. "Que linda familia!" notes Kathy. Roberto's mother smiles, but I believe I see a shadow of sadness momentarily eclipse her face. Roberto's father comes in from the kitchen and slouches into a chair while Roberto's mother does all the talking. Roberto laces his arms around his mother's neck lovingly. "How is my son behaving?" she asks. "He's great! I think he's starting to get used to me." Kathy responded.

. . .

Throughout the visit, Kathy and Roberto's mother continue to talk about how difficult the transition from second to third grade is. After spending two consecutive years with another teacher, it is difficult for Roberto to acclimate to a new teacher and a new environment. Kathy expresses her confidence in Roberto's abilities and assures his parents that "he'll come along."

. . .

"Well, I tell him that he needs to work hard in school so that he doesn't have to work in the field. It's really hard—really hard," adds Roberto's father, his eyes cast toward the floor. "Roberto says that you work in a floral shop" mentions Kathy to the mother. "I'm trying to get all the parents to come into the classroom and talk about their jobs and maybe give a lesson. Would you come teach my kids?" Roberto's mother seems pleased with Kathy's request. "Would you like your mom to come teach in the classroom, Roberto?" Kathy asks. Roberto answers with a nod and nestles closer to his mother.

. . .

A half-hour later, a young teenager comes out of one of the rooms. She is introduced as Mireya, Roberto's sister. Kathy asks her about school. Mireya exchanges nervous glances with her mother. "She is not in school right now. She's working in the fields with her father," interrupts her mother, "I tell her that she should finish school, but. . . . " "I don't have papers and . . . ," interjects Mireya. Her mother continues, "I tell her she should finish school because when I'm not here anymore, you don't know what will happen. You don't know if you end up with a husband that hits her and then she can't do anything." Kathy suggests that Mireya talk to the people in Migrant Education. "They will help you! I don't want to lecture you but you should really think about going back to school and finishing. You're almost there. That's all I'm going to say. I'll shut up now."

. . .

Throughout our conversation, I notice Roberto's brother peeking from behind a slightly opened door. Roberto's mother begins to share how "rough" Jose plays with

Roberto. "Sometimes too rough." I'm not sure how we got on to this topic. I sense some tension in the room. Without any warning, Roberto's father gets up and leaves the room. Roberto's mother invites us into the kitchen. She has prepared something "special" for us. Plates, carefully lined with fish tacos, await us on the kitchen table. Our conversation has moved through topics surrounding Roberto's education, Mireya's reentry to school, cooking, crocheting, dogs, money, boyfriends, etc. "I get a really good feeling from both of you. I feel like we've known each other longer," intimates Roberto's mother. I agree with her, musing over the family's openness toward Kathy and I. As our visit draws near its end, Kathy pulls out last year's class "Book of Families" containing all the family portraits and brief descriptions of every student in the class. "I need to take a picture when your dad comes back" says Kathy.

. . .

Roberto's father eventually returns and Kathy suggests that Roberto's brother also be in the picture. After much coaxing, Jose grudgingly emerges from the bedroom, only to quickly escape after the picture had been taken. Kathy and I are accompanied to the door. "Return whenever you please," assures the mother. As we pull out of the driveway, Roberto's mother is still standing on the porch. I can't help but notice the same lingering shadow in her expression, dulling her smile. I understood the nature of this shadow on the ride back home. I learned from Kathy that Roberto's father, an alcoholic, would frequently fall into violent moods and hit his wife. Jose, modeling his father's behavior, had also taken to beating on Roberto. Although many were still missing, the pieces of the puzzle gradually fell into place. I reflected on how threatening it might be for two strangers to come into their home, yet they had received us so openly. Both Kathy and I felt somewhat helpless over Roberto's family situation, but we were at least fueled by a determination to make Roberto's experience at school as positive as possible.

. . .

Roberto, who prior to the visit barely uttered two words to me, now comes and hugs me confidently. Since this last visit, Kathy has returned to Roberto's home for parent-teacher conferences and Roberto's birthday party. It is not surprising to me that, among all the teachers at the school, Kathy enjoyed the highest parent turnout on "Back-To-School-Night." Some of the arguments against doing home visits are that going into a family's home may be perceived as invasive. Throughout Kathy's last four years of teaching, she has never encountered any resistance when visiting her students' homes. I believe that the secret lies in "having no secrets" to a certain extent. It rests in the teacher's willingness to put aside all pretensions and reveal herself as equally human as her students and their families.

Marianna

"My Spanish is awful." This is my quiet confession to my master teacher as we near the front door. I am overcome by insecurities, entering someone else's home, their space. This is how my students must feel when they first come into my classroom, my space. Spaces where we do not all speak the same language. Nadeen knocks. I hold my breath. Alejandro answers, this is the student we have come to see, come to talk with. He is friendly, welcoming, and I am at a complete loss for words. His mother comes out of the kitchen carrying a tray full of *pan dulce*, and coffee, and hot sweet milk. We all sit and introduce ourselves. Alicia, Alejandro's mother, speaks no English, and Alejandro speaks very little. We begin by chatting, warming up our Spanish, talking about their lovely home and the delicious food.

. . .

Eventually we begin talking to Alejandro about his goals for the class. I realize that my Spanish is better than

I think, much better than I had anticipated. Alejandro expresses his concerns about the class: the material is too difficult on an English-Spanish level, but not quite hard enough to be intriguing on every other level. We then solicit ideas from Alejandro and his mother about materials which might be more interesting, yet more accessible. Alicia suggests many works in Spanish, but Nadeen tries to accentuate the need for the students' English skills to be developed as well.

. . .

When Alicia gets up to take the tray and cups back to the kitchen, I grab the basket of *pan* and follow along. In the kitchen Alicia seems a bit upset and I ask if she is okay. She confides that in Costa Rica she was a school teacher, a very educated woman with a career and intelligent children who were each reading (*en español*) by the time they were four. She is devastated now because here, in the U.S., she says that she is treated like dirt as though she is stupid or deaf. She is a maid at a local motel. The only thing she teaches, she says, is how to scrub toilets, and she only gets to do that when they hire a new maid. She cannot even help her children with their homework at night because she does not understand it. She said that she feels as dumb and useless as the White people around her perceive her to be.

. . .

I want desperately to stay there all night, talking about life here, and life in Costa Rica. Talking about language and privilege and stereotypes with this woman. I realize though as I hug her good-bye that I have learned more about education in one evening than I could in an entire quarter-long course. I used to feel that home visits were invasive, that it was wrong to take my White values and privilege into others' homes so that I could rat on their child. How interesting to me that I saw them in that light. Home visits, with families who are welcoming, are invasive primarily to the teacher's ideas, thought structures, and perceptions about students and families. The point is not to rat on the student; it's to get to know your student and their family, to let them get to know you. It is an interaction which, I feel, changes each of the participants in some way, simply by the sheer intimacy of the endeavor. I look forward to the opportunity to visit again.

As seen from these three encounters, home visits can alter the way veteran teachers and future teachers understand the larger context of their students' lives. It also provides a bridge, a neutral space, across which more authentic communication can flow. Teachers and parents are seen as real people whose lives are demanding and complex. Information about students that would normally be left unseen, untold, is often revealed, if not offered up, to the teacher as a sacrament in hopes that the child, in full array, will be understood, if not blessed, by the schooling process.

All teachers who have conducted home visits under my tutelage have claimed that their teaching would never be the same, that they would never be able to look at a child and make the same assumptions, and that they had radically altered their attitudes toward parents of color. Educational institutions, particularly those preparing teachers who do not place greater emphasis on creating opportunities and bridges for teachers to engage in the lives of students, are to be condemned.

CHAPTER 7

Deconstructing Youth At Risk

CREATING SAFE SPACES FOR URBAN VETERAN TEACHERS TO FACE UP TO their assumptions and stereotypes about the children they serve is one of the more difficult tasks I have confronted on a regular basis. In a class titled, "The Educational Challenges of Youth At Risk: Deconstructing Drop-outs," I introduced a means of intervention that served to transform not only the way educators viewed the community and students with whom they worked but also the way these educators situated themselves within the larger context of "at-riskness." To do this, I required my graduate students, all veteran educators, to conduct ethnographic fieldwork whereby their views on at-riskness became informed by a series of dialogues with students, staff, teachers, and administrators. The class took place in a city rich in diversity both in terms of socioeconomic class and ethnicity; however, the surrounding area is rural and has in recent years served as a bedroom community for professionals fleeing urban contexts. The course discussed here brought this contrast into vivid relief.

The research process required not only that the educators reevaluate their assumptions of at-riskness but also that they engage their students in conversations in ways that none of these seasoned educators had experienced before. While the process proved transformative for all concerned, it was not without risks. Exploring at-riskness in any depth has the potential of unleashing personal pain and closeted memory; confronting questions of confidentiality and trust is essential to the work.

Some of the more powerful results came from an examination of my graduate students' assumptions of at-riskness and their own personal encounters with marginality.

The other area of profound transformation came after they interviewed the students that they had assumed were at risk. In several cases, either these children were in fact not at risk of failure but simply fit the stereotypical criteria for at-riskness, or their marginality was due to an array of complex factors of which these teachers thus far had been ignorant. In all cases the teachers stated that thereafter they would never be able to view students in the same light and that their pedagogy had been changed forever. The reflective interviews transformed the way the teacher researchers viewed their students, their teaching, and themselves (Gordon, 2000c).

PROFILE OF STUDENT RESEARCHERS

All four of the students I have selected to highlight in this chapter were seasoned educators spanning a range of educational roles. The settings for their interviews differed dramatically from each other, providing valuable texture. Abby taught first grade in an inner-city school where the majority of students were low-income and African American. Dana, a high school principal, lived and worked in a rural community considered safe from the dangers of the city, but, as we learned, was not safe from the dangers of being at risk of failure. Brenda, on leave from teaching high school for twenty years, took advantage of her contacts and freedom from employment responsibilities to speak with a wide range of people across the district. Cathy, an education specialist at the state mental health hospital, provided us with an important perspective; the voices she shared sobered us to the reality that our actions can lead to unpredictable consequences.

All of the graduate students were White, female, and middle-class, though Dana and Brenda were raised in working-class homes and were first-generation college students. Part of the power of this project grew out of the interaction of professional White women working with predominately low-income students, a majority of whom were African American. None of the four women had been raised in a racially diverse environment and yet each perceived herself able and willing to work with the youth of inner-city schools. As the course progressed, the women came to realize how different their upbringing was from those of their students and how their upbringing contributed to attitudes and beliefs toward their students that limited their work as teachers.

THE COURSE

I had four objectives for this course:

1. demythologize the concept of at-riskness;
2. define what contributes to students' apparent school failure;
3. identify interventions and changes in traditional schooling that could prevent withdrawal from school; and
4. get my teacher graduate students in touch with youth and families who needed help.

Knowing that all but one of the students were full-time educators and had little time to study, I paced the course purposely to ensure progressive and coherent quality work. I constructed a set of topics, inquiries, and readings to guide their weekly interviews. My hope was that by having all students working with a similar population on the same questions but in different contexts, they would be able to provide multiple perspectives on at-riskness. Weekly assignments required their personal responses as well as transcriptions of parts of the interviews that applied to the topic under discussion. Each seminar session allowed for airing of problems as well as comparison of interview results within the assigned population for the week.

The weekly instructions were as follows:

Week I. Examine your own assumptions about at-riskness. Where do these ideas come from? What experiences have shaped these views?

Week II. Interview teachers, counselors, administrators, janitors, and secretaries to find out how at-riskness is defined at school. For example, are at-risk students identified by attitude, clothing, home environment, learning problems, and/or low grades?

Week III. Identify four or five students who meet your criteria for at-riskness. Explain your reasons for the choice.

Week IV. Begin interviews with the students you identified as at-risk in Week III.

Week V. Discuss with students in the classroom where you teach the definition of at-riskness and inquire about their reasons.

Week VI. Interview counselors and teachers regarding how the families of at-risk youth are perceived.

Week VII. Interview administrators as to the institutional response to at-riskness. Inquire about the relationship between at-riskness and dropping-out.

Week VIII. Based on your research, present what you see as a valid justification for kids staying in school.

As a final project, student researchers wrote a reflective report on their findings that included their own transformations. The outcomes of the students' research provided valuable illustrations of how educators working with "youth at-risk" understand their work and how those same youth understand their situations with school.

This chapter focuses first on an examination of my students' *assumptions* concerning at-riskness as well as a discussion of their personal encounters with marginality and, second, on a discussion of how the interactive, *reflective* interviews *transformed* the way the student researchers viewed their students, their teaching, and themselves.

LOCATING THE SELF IN MARGINALITY

Masks of graduate student appropriateness melted quickly in the seminar when I probed beneath the students' veiled language of at-riskness. Continually asking for the decoding of a particular word or idea, I realized that their first definitions of what it meant to be at-risk were far from what they really believed and far from what they could document. In many ways they had internalized the acceptable response to the pat question of "how would you identify at-riskness?" In order to proceed, I needed to know what stereotypes or experiences they were accessing. How much did they believe what they claimed? How open would they be to new definitions? With cautious constraint they began listing the typical litany of indicators for at-riskness: single parent, low income, visible minority status other than Asian, drugs and/or alcohol addiction, English as a second language, teen pregnancy, as so on. For each comment I asked for further clarification and the basis of their opinion. It was not long before they joined me in the process, winnowing out their preconceptions, based on the media or mythology, from their actual experience.

I was concerned that some of them had come from sheltered, middle-class, monocultural backgrounds and might be jumping to conclusions regarding low-income children of color. My fear was only partially unfounded. As I read Abby's responses it became clear that she was definitely working with kids who were struggling. While I cringed at her accusation that "these children are victims of their home environment," she had numerous examples from her first-grade classroom to back up her assumption:

> Bobby lost his mother when his father shot her. Charmaine, a crack baby, lives with her mother who is a prostitute. Marimo has had trouble sleeping because of the constant ringing of gunshots in the neighborhood. Carrie comes to school in dirty clothes that often smell of urine. Rosie got lost walking to school alone on the first day of first grade. Jesse's mother had been in jail three times by the time he started school. Carla has asked for extra apples and oranges to take home because her mom sometimes forgets to buy food.

Abby reported, "I had no difficulty identifying four at-risk children to interview, I could have selected forty (the total enrollment)." Without invalidating Abby's claims I wanted to broaden the definition of at-riskness. Coming from a small rural middle-class community to a low-income inner-city school without any preparation for transitioning, Abby appeared trapped in a form of shell shock where every story confirmed her wildest nightmares. Since I had worked with White middle-class students who were severely at risk and in alternative dropout programs, as well as with inner-city youth, I needed to provide her with some breadth. It was not long before the experiences of the other graduate students gave her new lenses through which to view her situation. As the trust level increased, so did the revelations. Gradually, the women in the class challenged the traditional perception of at-riskness, citing cases of marginality within their own middle-class schools and communities. Their readiness to debunk the mythologies led me to wonder if these women themselves had tales that could match some of Abby's students' stories; I had no idea to what degree I was correct.

One of the most reserved and conservative students, Cathy, lingered after the first class and thanked me for being so candid about my own life history and challenging them to see beyond the "masks of normality." She then, haltingly, revealed her own life of at-riskness within a family where appearances were of utmost importance. Raised in an elite, midwestern family, she was sexually abused as a child and sent to a psychiatrist at age four. Her father, a leading doctor in the Midwest, moved the family across country to the West Coast when she was ten years old. One week after settling into their exclusive new neighborhood, he committed suicide. All the funeral arrangements had been made prior to his leaving his old town. No one had suspected anything. Cathy wrote,

> From that time on, my life became a litany of "at-risk" behaviors: social phobia, molestation by a teacher, teen-age pregnancy, dropping out of school, early marriage, rape, drugs, and divorce. But what teacher would have called the quiet, good student from a seemingly perfect home with wealthy, well-educated parents an "at-risk child"? I was not a threat to society. Few people, and no teachers,

knew I was in pain. In my family we did not tell the truth; denial of truth, even to oneself, was like a virtue. Silencing often begins at home.

I asked Cathy if she would share her story with the class. She claimed she wanted to, and needed to, but was afraid. The next week she handed me a six-page paper and asked if she could read her version of children at-risk to the class. Head lowered, she read word for word. Never looking up, she did not see the tears on the faces of her classmates. She had crossed a watershed.

Over the next few weeks each of the other women in the class shared her tale of at-riskness. Brenda, a well-to-do executive's wife and veteran teacher, revealed that she had a son, Jonathan, who "puts us all at risk, emotionally and physically." She wrote, "I have two definitions of the term 'at risk': one of the textbook and one of the heart." Later in her interviews with other educators who knew her only as an outstanding, respected veteran teacher, she heard constantly, "These kids [at risk] aren't like ours, are they Brenda? They don't have intact families; there's no structure; they're poor, take drugs." In her heart she knew a different reality. One of her best friend's son, Robert, was severely at risk. Since having been told that his father had terminal cancer, Robert had refused to function at school. Internalizing the anger and guilt, he was silent, scarring himself physically and emotionally, his future precariously hinged on how he dealt with the loss.

Dana, the fourth student researcher, represented a case of split siblings in which one, Dana, was a socially acceptable success and the other, her brother, she claimed was "lost to society." As a first-generation college student, she had moved through the local community college and regional normal school to return to teach and later become principal of the same high school from which she graduated. Her brother, on the other hand, followed a different track. She wrote, "It is difficult to believe that my brother and I were raised in the same family because our values concerning education are so opposite. My brother's attitude is that the world owes him something." Her concern was that her brother's rejection of education and his marriage to a woman

who had not finished high school set a pattern of oppositional behavior for their children who had dropped out of school in their
early teens. Frustrated with a sense of inadequacy, Dana's papers to me frequently revisited issues of guilt and impotence.
When confronted with a marginalized student at her school, she
would ask herself, "Did I do enough? Where did I go wrong? How
could I have averted the situation? Why didn't I see it coming?" I
could not help wondering how much she was projecting onto her
students her own concern and confusion for her brother.

TRANSFORMATIVE PRAXIS

Perceptual transformation. While all of these student researchers
had had extensive experience with youth, including those at risk,
nothing quite prepared them for the knowledge that they received during the interviews. Prior to this research they had been
able to distance themselves from the realities of their students'
lives through their *role* as teacher. Abby wrote of her experience:

> The interviews themselves were not shocking. These are
> my children; I knew their experiences before the inter-
> views. I had been desensitized. It was not until I typed
> their voices into the computer that I let myself feel what
> was happening, what they go through every day. It is so
> important to remember how young they are [1st graders]
> and what lives they have led so far. They know so much.

Sitting down with students one on one provided a level of intimacy that dissolved the traditional barriers of hierarchy and
power so often associated with teacher-student relations (Apple,
1982). Several of the student researchers confessed that while
they taught students every day, they seldom honestly talked *with*
their students. They talked to them, disciplined them, cajoled
them, and encouraged them, but they did not take the time to sit
down and talk *with* them in a context where the teacher became
the learner, the listener. After learning that the vast majority of
her informants between the ages of sixteen and eighteen years
were working twenty-five to thirty hours a week and that some

were juggling two jobs, Dana wrote the following: "Kids are not irresponsible as I had always presumed; they are hyper responsible. These are the survivors. They have lived through experiences that I can't even begin to imagine and they have learned to accept their life, their past, and take each day as it comes."

Brenda came to a similar conclusion after several interviews with students who had dropped out. Their reasons for leaving had less to do with academic failure than with boredom or fear of returning to a unsafe, unfriendly environment. For some of the young women she interviewed, the stigma of pregnancy was humiliating. One young woman who had dropped out at fifteen was rearing a family on her own. A male who left at sixteen lived out of his car while studying for his G.E.D. Another lad, seventeen years old, while supporting his wife and child, lost his minimum wage job at "Pay and Pack" because of downsizing.

The inmates at the mental health facility whom Cathy interviewed were an extension of the stories above. Ninety percent of her informants claimed a direct connection between their K–12 experiences and their current condition. She wrote: "My findings demonstrate that the mental and emotional problems that lead people to be committed to State Hospital begin during the school years and that the response of school personnel to these problems is harmful rather than helpful."

In hearing excerpts from some of the inmates' stories one cannot help wondering how educators might have responded differently. Inmate A dropped out in the sixth grade: "I tried to return but the other students kept calling me retarded." Inmate B's anger-control problem was the result of being badly mistreated at school on account of her facial disfigurement. Inmate C left school in the ninth grade because "the principal was a bastard who paddled people." Inmate C never learned to read. Inmate D, who got his G.E.D. at the state penitentiary, transferred his skills from prankster to tough guy after a teacher scolded him in the seventh grade for playing the class clown: "He put me in the hot seat and it changed my life. I couldn't laugh after that; I was very shy. I didn't know how to talk to people." He was expelled for possession of a deadly weapon. Inmate E's parents, both college graduates, had high expectations for their children before alcoholism scarred their parental sanity. Frequent fights and abuse brought their daughter to declare herself mentally ill by her senior year. She described her life as "running in a maze."

Pedagogical transformation. During the interviews multiple transformations took place. The student "informants" became aware that their teacher was genuinely interested in what they had to say. Teacher researchers realized either that they had been working from false assumptions about the students they had labeled at risk or that they had misinterpreted a child's call for help. Abby elaborated on this point:

> Interviewing gave me a chance to spend individual time with each student. Time is something that they desperately need. They felt important, as if their teacher really cared about them. Of course I do care, but I often forget the importance of short talks with them. The interviews showed me that I can never forget where these kids come from. They come to school hurting and teachers must understand that. Interviews are important for every teacher with every student. After this assignment I began having "talks" with all my students.

Out of this research came an increased respect for the opinions, decisions, and social analysis of the youth, given their limited options. Most students understood the economic, political, and social context that had placed their parents, and therefore them, at risk. While the majority of the adult staff who were interviewed blamed parents and the home life, the students did not. If anything, they felt their parents placed a very high degree of value on education. The reality that parents might not know how to translate this into support was a separate issue. Similarly, in identifying the characteristics of youth at risk, the gap between adult perception and student perception was significant. Students were far more attuned to the subtle signs of at-riskness than were the adults, who were responsible for prevention and intervention. Adults used external factors such as clothing and hairstyles or apathy toward schoolwork as signifiers. Youth, in contrast, were quick to discredit these blatant characteristics, noting that it is often the "perfect student" who is most at risk. As one sixteen-year-old girl put it, "The eyes reveal the pain." Students had little use for the popular term "attention deficit," claiming that there was a fine line between those who choose to do the work and those who do not. Explaining the difference between her and a student at risk, Michelle, a middle school student, commented, "I do the work, even if it is dumb; they don't."

Shocked by the realization that years of frustration and misinformation could have been alleviated had they created spaces in which to listen to students, these educators began to reshape their pedagogy, increase their outreach to guardians, and rethink their priorities. All claimed that they could never again teach in the same way as they had done in the past. Dana wrote, "We have to listen to the voices of our students. In many cases they see the issues of at-riskness more clearly than the adults who are trying to find solutions." Abby came to the same conclusion, "To understand the school, the stories of the children must be heard."

Personal transformation. The opportunity to talk with students, staff, faculty, parents, and community members under the guise of a required class assignment enabled these student researchers (though veteran teachers) not only to access information to which they might not otherwise be privy but also to access silent or hidden parts of themselves. For most, this was the first time that they had been in such a powerful yet vulnerable position. Inquiries, couched in the context of research, appeared less threatening to both their colleagues and students. One of the researchers prefaced her interview questions to a group of sophomores by explaining that this was an assignment for her graduate class and stated, "I need your help with my homework." Students, taken by the idea that even their teacher was under pressure to produce results for her professor, gathered around and offered their responses to questions of how one identifies students at risk. Colleagues who previously appeared impervious or aloof offered up their frustration and suggestions;

recalcitrant students willingly discussed their reasons for resisting the system; parents divulged their confusion and anger.

Cathy, who had remained in a relatively passive position at
her job, became an advocate for student rights, while intending
to continue her research and pursue advanced training. In her
final paper she wrote:

> In analyzing and responding to the demands for change,
> the objective, anthropological stance used in ethnographic
> research could be an approach that preserves my sanity.
> On-going research, analysis of observations, and frequent
> reflection will hopefully help me cope with the accelerating
> pace of change while retaining the positive influence I now
> have on students' lives.

Abby claimed that one interview, in particular, provided her
with a powerful reminder of why she became a teacher. In talking about her problems at school, Betsy, a first-grader, shared
with Abby that she had been "hurt" by "an uncle" but had not
told anyone. Even though Abby knew that the girl had been mo-
lested before, she did not expect her to bring forth this information. The child's response did not relate to anything that Abby
had said to the child. The next day Betsy's mother came to
school and Abby was called into the principal's office. The
mother asked Abby what she had done to get her daughter to
open up and speak so freely. Apparently, Betsy had gone home
and told her mom that she and her teacher had had a talk and
when the mother asked what about, she told her. The mother
was grateful to Abby for creating a safe space for her daughter to
speak candidly. She had long suspected that Betsy had been sub-
jected to abuse and had noted a change in her daughter's dispo-
sition a year earlier but had been unable to get her to talk about
it. Abby said at the end of her reflective paper that week: "I had
forgotten the enormous influence teachers can have on children's
lives; Betsy reminded me. This is why I went into teaching."

The general consensus among my students held that perhaps
what prevented educators from involvement in the lives of their
students was a feeling of powerlessness: the awareness that sim-

plistic quick fixes would not remove a child from poverty, from abuse, or from discrimination. Yet, these student researchers concluded that their involvement had moved them toward greater commitment. Knowledge of their students and the communities in which they lived gave them a strength and confidence they previously were unaware they could even hope to attain. Upon reflection, Cathy recommended that we provide more opportunities for teachers to access their students' lives: "Just as we allow for children to learn through small successes, we need to let teachers to do the same thing. Often we forget the impact we can have on children's lives. One way to help 'at-risk' children succeed is to help 'at-risk' teachers. The solutions for helping 'at-risk students' exist in connection to the student's family."

CHAPTER 8

Adult Educators Inquire into Workplace Stress

WHAT ARE THE ETHICAL ISSUES INVOLVED IN PARTICIPATING IN THE EDU-cation and retraining of adult learners who have been relieved of their jobs because of downsizing and subcontracting? As teacher educators, how do we respond to the needs of people who are already well-educated, some with master's degrees? How do we conduct a social foundations class for individuals who are astutely aware of the economic conspiracy of capitalism and have held prestigious and responsible positions only to have their jobs jerked away when they fall victim to injury or accident or by someone else's greed? By leading them on to assume that education in any form will ensure a more secure future, are we not collaborating with a pretense that has already undermined their sense of self?

Teaching an adult education course in a large city known for its sophisticated, diverse, and politically aware population has its own challenges and rewards. While the course title "The Psychology and Sociology of Education" was generic and the design served as a core seminar for graduate students in the first year of a traditional master's program, I have always modified the content to respond to the type of students I anticipated I would be teaching. Alhough I had worked with older, well-educated, urban students who enjoyed challenging authority and leveling the hierarchy so endemic to education, I had not taught a group of students all of whom had either been laid off or were in fear of losing their jobs in nonprofit or government agencies and institutions. They saw themselves as educators but not in the traditional school/classroom context.

Downsizing, disability, depression, and depressants brought unlikely folk together for a quarter to begin work on a master's degree that they hoped would provide them with a new life or a new way to face their old life. Skeptical, these people did not want to form a "learning community." Burned by the capitalist forces that drive modern urban life, my students provided me with more sufficient work for the course; however, I wondered whether they would collaborate in the effort. Unemployed or in fear of that prospect, my students had returned to college to reorient and retool for work in academia. Two of the students had become disabled and lost their jobs. One of these had gradually become blind over the last ten years. These were bright, working-class individuals who, by circumstances having little to do with their ability, were being marginalized. Some had not been in school for twenty years and had little patience for traditional schooling or for theories that did not match reality. The majority had suffered at the hands of institutional schooling and had rebelled, opting for drugs or alcohol or marriage as an escape from the reality of prostituting themselves to an unreliable and unforgiving job market. They were skeptical about the course and what they could possibly learn from it or me. I knew that to keep these streetwise, work-abused, and middle-aged professionals engaged I had to make the issues that related to their immediate lives central to the course.

My formal task was to get them through the first course of a two-year degree program with the hope that they would return the following quarter. The assignments for the course included a detailed self-portrait that focused on economic factors and prior job experience as well as weekly presentations in which a small group of students would lead the discussion based on their extended readings and would make linkages to their work/life/ school situation. In addition to an introduction to interviewing as an approach to critical ethnography and the reading of Michael Lerner's *Surplus Powerlessness* (1992) and R. D. Laing's *Politics of the Family* (1969), the major assignment was a case study looking at work as an educational setting through the eyes of an educator. I asked the students to use observation, interviews, and analysis in their research and to apply the concepts presented in the readings. My original intention was to ask them to look at workplace transformations in urban areas and the resulting displacement of workers. After brainstorming possible interview questions, we decided to consider a more specific aspect of the workplace; stress and its effect on performance. The crucial part of the course became their interviews with co-workers, past or present, concerning sources of stress and ways of managing stress at both work and home.

This chapter both studies the transformative process of adult educators who have interviewed their co-workers about workplace stress and explores how people can address problems of stress through professional development. The key to the success of this type of work is found in the experience of the ethnographic interview on the part of both interviewer and interviewee. In the case study, both participants shared a workplace. The stresses identified in the interviews were often common for both individuals. The interview thus became a source of support and insight concerning workplace stress for both. Some students asked if they could go back to their old positions and conduct the interviews. Others relished the idea of investigating the causes of potential downsizing at their jobs. Still others were curious to talk with co-workers about the connection between stress and productivity. As conversations evolved, feelings of isolation dissolved.

The link between home stress and work stress became apparent at the very beginning. Students began to reevaluate their current employment crisis and noted how it affected their relationships with friends and families. Over the course of the quarter, radical changes occurred, not at my initiative but from the process of honest inquiry itself. Some students began calling their adult children to talk about the issues raised in the course readings about family dynamics, often sharing copies of the textbooks as well. Other students talked about the course with partners, spouses, and friends. Home life and work life became fertile ground for quality discussion and epiphanies. The students came to feel more in control of their situation and less victimized as they came to understand through the interviews the complexity of causes for the stress and resulting changes in work patterns. In one case a male office worker found that people whom he interviewed began telling others about the process, and colleagues, who had previously never spoken to him, wanted to share their perspective on his research topic. On the last day of class, to the astonishment of all, another male student said that he had quit his job of eighteen years at a prestigious university because he had identified it as the main source of his stress, his estrangement from his wife, and resultant alcoholism.

The range of research sites provided a rich layering of experience shared each week in class. The sites included community colleges, unions, a Veterans Affairs office, a prison, an environmental agency, the State Division of Vocational Rehabilitation, a chemical dependency rehabilitation facility, a university staff position, a computer company, a JTPA (Job Training Project Act) counseling program, a state parks and recreation office, Head Start Administration, and K–12 schools. The results of the research were fascinating, and the intervention through critical ethnography was transformative on multiple levels.

STUDENT PROFILES AND SAMPLES OF THEIR PROJECTS IN THEIR OWN WORDS

I tend to gravitate toward the student who seems to have the most potential but due to anger or fear will not give an inch. I remember these students best as they become my "projects." They are my canary in the coal mine. If I can turn them around, I know that my work has not been in vain. Sometimes I have several of these in a class, but usually there is one most in need. In this class there were three, but Travis was the most recalcitrant and as such became a ring leader. I knew if I wanted to remain credible to this group, I would have to gain his trust and respect. One evening he spoke to me before class about his friend, Mark, who had just gotten out of prison and had dropped by his house wanting to stay for a while, much to his wife's chagrin. Travis went on to say that during their long natter over booze and cigarettes, Mark asked him how it was that Travis's life had turned out so well. Both of them had been imprisoned at the same time for committing a crime. Travis had gotten two years, Mark eighteen. Travis, forty years old, a not-so-well recovered alcoholic, and into his third marriage, had never seen his life as being much more than a sham held together by lies and impersonations.

Travis worked at a local university as an administrator in student services. The quality of his interviews demonstrated the trust and confidence that he had established with the staff and students with whom he worked. The range of their pain and confusion of their lives was astounding, but he recognized its validity and the need for it to be heard by a larger audience. Travis's final presentation set the tone that I had been searching for all quarter. I thought it would never come as he and most of the other students seemed so resistant, not to me, but to the process of making the connections. Here is a portion of Travis's final written report:

This quarter, this project, and my internship at CC where I decided to conduct my interviews have had a profound effect on me. I am now an "expert" on the world of work! I observe and experience daily the powerlessness of the working class. I see this powerlessness increasing. A worker can no longer rely on his/her seniority. Employers want educated people who can make decisions and solve problems. Entry level jobs require literacy. Keep up or get out! Looking at my small sample, I would say family dysfunction is the number one source of powerlessness and surplus powerlessness in our society. Not one of my informants noted family as a primary means of stress reduction. Family is the main source of what Lerner calls toxic stress for this group.

. . .

What strikes me most about being back in school [after having been working for 18 years], whether you are good or bad at it, is how empowering it is. It is not just knowledge that empowers. Going to school is the number one, socially accepted, pursuit in the dominant culture. I am also struck by how little powerlessness school generated. There was stress, but it is school stress and everybody has it. You can be proud of it. Sharing my personal experience in this class, conducting this research through my counseling practicum, and visiting with old friends have put me in touch with surplus powerlessness I hadn't really yet identified. After class Tuesday night I decided that the source of my toxic stress was my job as an administrator. Wednesday I quit! Immediate relaxation response. I also found something I really like; something I am really good at. I talked to a lot of students this quarter as a result of these interviews and did a lot of counseling. You would have been proud, June. I just reached out and engaged my students. It was way past cool.

Charlotte, who had a mild but engaged demeanor, was probably the best student in terms of quality and consistency of work. Her final report had all the makings of a publishable article. Her research site, a rehabilitation center, provided her with insights into the lives of the inmates and their keepers as well as the conditions that set the stage for the performance of respective roles. At first frightened by the situation, she gradually relaxed as she gained the informants' trust. Her report exposed how job security contributed to the status of prisons as one of the few growth industries in this state. She found it ironic that people who had endured the stress of losing a job would find pleasure in their work, even within prison walls. Charlotte's report included the following:

The North Rehabilitation Facility is a minimum security drug and alcohol rehabilitation facility. The assistant administrator has experience of just four months at this facility and is part of the "new guard" that began here in January. The stress of being in a new work situation was definitely acknowledged in his interview, and the ramifications of it on his home life indicate that he has been doing a fair amount of reflection about this issue and its effects. But he is highly educated and skilled and is one of those who has more choices and options about how he chooses to deal with his stress level. He obviously believes in the ability to change, and his description of his reasons for being in government echoes Lerner's idea of public sector employees' "reclaiming [although this guy has not lost it!] the idealism and positive energy that led them to their jobs in the first place."

. . .

The employment development specialist (EDS) is a highly educated Black man who exudes positive energy and enthusiasm. One aspect of his interview that I found particularly interesting was as [sic] he discussed parts of his job that he didn't enjoy as much as others. His description of residents "who have been in and out of jail so much that they become institutionalized in their thinking" made me think about this as almost a parallel to Lerner's idea of surplus powerlessness and the idea that we can pay lip service but actually may give up on change because there is a part of us that has accepted the notion of futility and internalized it. In the case of recidivists, the idea of self-worth and self blame would be especially revealing.

. . .

The interview with a Security Detention Supervisor (SDA) was one of the most insightful that I had. In his late twenties to early thirties, this man spoke about his job in a genuinely more compassionate way than anyone else that I talked to. This was definitely one of the surprises of this project. His emphasis on his ability to relate to the residents (having lived through some abuse himself) and respect them as individuals, while acknowledging that he was in a position of control impressed me. He was one person who honestly admitted that this was a stressful and horribly negative environment to work in, and his struggle with that appears to be ongoing. His sense of responsibility and duty to do one's job well also seemed to weigh heavily.

Rob, an angry environmental anarchist and avid biker with a sordid history of heavy drugs, worked, though not very effectively, at an occupational rehab center. Cynical to the point of being ignored by his peers, he wanted to be seen as a loner in an arrogant way. Different from Travis whose cynicism provided him with leadership and clown qualities, Rob was more frightening in his quietness. He was capable of being very articulate but also mean-spirited. When I read the final words of his report, I felt that we, as a class, had accomplished a great deal: "As a result of this course, I have developed more respect and compassion for my co-workers." Here is a snapshot from the summary of his research of how this came about.

It quickly became apparent to me that when people feel out of control, or in Lerner's word, powerless, they are able to access feelings within them that seem rather powerful. Of course, this assumes that my presence had no impact on S, and we know that idea to be wrong. Could it be that my presence impacted (empowered?) S in a similar way to the Occupational Stress Groups empowerment of people by providing a safe context for people to learn about the ways that stress is rooted in their environment . . . and legitimate working people's anger at oppressive work conditions?

I found the process of analyzing these interviews to really be illuminating. I recognized things people were telling me that I am not sure either of us were aware of at the time. This information is a lot stronger than I first suspected. I know this project has offered far more to me than I first would have guessed. I think I learned a lot about the process of interviewing a person as I gained experience. Thus, my last interview was the one I liked the best. I think this skill might encourage me to become involved with interviews more as a way to get feedback than I might otherwise have. I also learned new time management skills. I'm glad I followed your advice of doing at least one a week from the beginning. I found it real interesting that after all the colored pens I used to recognize the themes between the interviews, when I actually sat down to compile and analyze the findings—this paper wrote itself. Really.

Nora, a codirector of Head Start for the county, was used to being in charge and prided herself in "not putting up with any shit." Nora wanted to control conversation and at the beginning made it unsafe for others in the class, particularly shy women, to risk sharing their ideas. While she railed against hierarchy and advocated for a more "feminist" view of learning, she lacked an awareness of how she intimidated others. I shared these perceptions with her in order for her to reexamine the issue of power and control. Nora's response was measured and forthright as she opted to change the direction of her research to explore how these factors played out in her current workplace where she shared administrative authority. She wrote the following in her final report:

> [after the interviews] I was impressed that while the teachers viewed their work as valuable, they did not view their work as valued, since there was so little public support for making needed change. All but one teacher (the associate teacher) mentioned the classroom as a place of satisfaction, power, and transformation: The classroom is a powerful place. It's a place from which teachers derive their sense of self as a professional, their sense of worth in spite of low wages and social status, their sense of control.
>
> All seven teachers interviewed indicated that they dealt with work situations or stresses that they wished to change, but over which they had little or no power to change. Some teachers indicated that they dealt with dissatisfactions in their work life outside the classroom by focusing on the life of the classroom. As one teacher said, "I see people use 'power over' when they don't know that they have the 'power within'—trying to control what's outside because you don't have the power inside."

Steve was the large, friendly but resistant student. He worked as one of several employment and training counselors in a small office space underneath a parking garage for an agency facing stiff competition for contracts amidst decreasing federal funds. Steve's training was client-centered therapy and he proved an able listener. His interviewees explored a range of questions relating to work, home, life, efforts to change stress, and so on. He found a split between well-paid old-timers and insecure newcomers. The old-timers had less stress and ease of getting work while the newcomers felt isolated and blamed circumstances for their stress. This connection between maturity and fear of job loss echoed throughout his interviews.

During the personal interviews, the information gathered was very terse and pithy. I can only assume that there was a little trepidation felt at giving personal information to a rather new, big hairy guy. During the later interviews, new information could be attained due to a reference being made to a previous group discussion topic. What was even more apparent was that my participation in the group discussions may have caused me to be looked upon more favorably as the latter interviews did increase in comfort level. Once the conversations began, new information was extracted due to one person bringing up a subject that all the others had experienced. This allowed for a significant amount of discussion on a shared stress. This discussion seemed to actually alleviate some of the stress they were talking about. In effect, these little interviews became something of a support group. The vast majority of the time these small groups were made up of all women, except for me, of course. Most of the time, they made statements to the effect of their significant others adding stress in their lives rather than relieving stress. The men apparently put added requirements on the time of the women rather than being supportive. The women reported a tremendous amount of selfishness among the men. When the men needed the women, the women were expected to be there. But when the women needed the men, the men were there depending on whether or not their favorite show was on. The women expressed a significant amount of anger over this double standard. Interestingly enough, none of the women even considered seeking out a mate that would be more suitable. I suppose what I wasn't privy to was the behaviors the men expressed that the women did appreciate.

Jenny, crazy Jenny, unable to justify her manliness with her giddiness, remained in an ambivalent state until she realized that we did not really care how she presented herself. An excellent student handicapped by huge gaps in her education, she strained over the material, foreign to her until illuminated by her peers or myself. Starved for validation and support, she worked tirelessly to prove herself equal to those she admired. Jenny conducted a very powerful set of interviews at the community college where she worked:

I have known all of the people I interviewed for a number of years. Some I have known on a very personal level, others I've known only in the realm of the workplace. Because the level of trust, as I perceived it, is at low ebb, I chose to interview all but two of these people at my home. It is proximal [sic] to the college and as such posed little inconvenience to the subjects of my study. This also provided some measure of privacy which was extremely important to their comfort in answering my questions. While it was my intention to survey persons representative of different areas and levels of responsibility, I think it is worthy to note that I did not feel comfortable speaking to any of the higher-level administrators and felt it necessary to try to protect the interests of the persons surveyed by keeping this project quiet. One of the most saddening things I came to understand from this process is the erosion of confidence I perceived in these people. These are competent, experienced people who are doing a good job and enjoy their work for the most part. But they do not feel the security that knowing you do a good job should bring. It is not just that they don't have any power within the decision-making process. They feel buffeted about by the whims of the administration. Rather than feeling that the decisions of the leadership contribute to providing better service for the students, it's another millstone to be carried while trying to do the work that needs doing.

. . .

The attributes which make the college a desirable employer also serve to entrap people in their own powerlessness. The velvet handcuffs which keep people working in this system are things like medical plans, retirement pensions, paid vacations, and sick leave, all the trappings of "secure" work. The prices these people are paying for these amenities are much higher than they perceive on a conscious level. They are paying with their health in some cases, in others self-esteem and personal values are spent for the sake of other goals. Choices are made according to the personal priorities of each to bring about results in the most satisfactory way they know according to the lessons that have brought them to where they are today. I harbor a great deal of hope for our college because people such as those I interviewed have weathered other brainstorms. No matter what "the administration" does, the students still come, they still need our help to access their educational experiences, and they are still, after all, "the work that needs doing."

Tamara brought out my sternest comments both to her and to fellow students who took advantage of her reticence to speak out. As we all discovered, she had a lot to say and provided one of the more thoroughgoing applications of Lerner's concept of surplus powerlessness. Tamara, in her own words:

After completing my interviews I found that the counselors' responses were not only similar to each other but also similar to what Lerner says in his book, particularly with regard to the Chapter on Anger. The counselors at the facility all expressed that there are many aspects of their jobs which caused them to have severe stress which resulted in their having both emotional and physical prob-

lems. These included dealing with the guilt of client re-
lapse, overwhelming paperwork, no support from Management and fear of losing their positions. The counselors
found themselves internalizing these negative feelings
which eventually led to anger, frustration, guilt, and self-
blame. Their anger and frustration which they internalized at work unfortunately was released at home which
ultimately caused very destructive consequences for them.
For example, one counselor vented her anger at her children which eventually resulted in their having emotional
problems. One counselor who said he was so stressed out
from work that he began to isolate himself from his four-
year old son who lives with him on weekends. Two of the
counselors, who at one time in their life used and abused
drugs and alcohol started to isolate themselves socially.
The counselors also started to develop problems physically
which included over-eating which led to high blood pressure problems for one counselor, a return to smoking and a
discontinuance of an exercise program which resulted in a
20 pound weight gain for two other counselors. Eventually
all of the counselors, although through no encouragement
of Management, sought some type of outside help such as
group therapy, individual therapy and/or stress management groups which unfortunately did not eliminate their
problems, but it certainly helped them to redirect their
anger and frustration into more positive ways preferably
through action.

Gilda was the most feisty among a generally lively group. Her
project was a fascinating case study of how management can un-
dercut their employees by keeping them stressed and distrustful
of each other. Her project report begins with her decision to return to her old workplace for interviews.

This writer worked for the department of vocational rehabilitation as a vocational counselor for more then five
years. Although, no longer employed with DVR, it is my

memory of constant frustration, unbridled anxiety and absolute bewilderment of the boundless means this system, and the management therein, has in place that unconscionably truncate and denigrate professional adults (vocational counselors) in their effort to perform their jobs. During the span of 5 years of employment with DVR, I experienced ubiquitous discontent by employees manifested in varying degrees of depression, anxiety, one psychotic break with resulting hospitalization and rampant paranoia. More than half of the employees within the three offices in my area were on antidepressants and had chronic stress-related illnesses such as stomach disorders and headaches. Marital distress was a constant focus of discussion and frequent instances of infidelity occurred resulting in dissolution of marriage and/or other partnerships on more then one occasion. Predicated on my history and comradely [sic] with this battle-weary group, whom [sic] routinely shared intimate feelings of professional and personal demise in their emotional struggle with their job and their life, I am compelled to return to these folks as the focus of this analysis—just as I had often in my mind when reading Lerner and R. D. Laing.

Delores was probably the most "normal" person in the group. Not sane like Charlotte but normal in her middle-class life and concerns. Yet, to my surprise, when it came to a research topic she selected bilingual education and went after the complexities of the issue with a vengeance. Excerpts from Delores' report follow:

The big picture that emerged from the interviews was that of fear, distrust, and powerlessness. Inclusion happened *to* them. They were not a part of the adoption process, they never bought into it, they fought it. In some cases they won, but not without substantial division among staff and administration. The divisiveness of the project fed on already existing patterns of distrust among staff. The end product, for most, was stress-induced physical and emotional problems and an increased sense of powerlessness. The workplace for some of these teachers is a place to exercise caution. Camps have formed over issues, such as Inclusion, and one's allegiance determines whom it is safe to talk to. One is always looking over one's shoulder while treading carefully to protect one's job. A sense of powerlessness flows from the fear that overt disagreement will result in termination.

. . .

The sense of powerlessness is not only generated by fear for one's job. It is further cemented by the imposition of the Inclusion Model without the input of the people who would be implementing it. Most of the teachers interviewed felt they had no say in their school's adoption of Inclusion. Their sense of powerlessness in the face of this decision ultimately manifested itself in disaffection with the program. They had seen many such improvement programs come and go over the years and had developed a skepticism about any new program's life expectancy. In addition, most of those interviewed have as yet an unclear understanding of Inclusion itself, several years into the program.

Phyllis was a self-declared tomboy, good natured, and much younger than her current classmates. In her words:

When describing stress and how it manifests itself in the work setting, participants mentioned two issues: interpersonal relationships and excessive work loads. I consider this part of surplus powerlessness that is created on the job. This surplus powerlessness is created by the individuals and the departmental demands upon them. Lerner talks about physical and medical manifestations of stress. There are several examples of this from my sample. J is the most obvious representation of stress taking a toll on her body. She gets sores all over her body, she has stomach ailments, insomnia, and now cancer from stress. She knows that if she were to exercise and eat right she would feel better, but she does not have the time to do these simple things for herself; I would venture to say that she does not allow herself to relax. She is either working at the Center or socializing with her friends and boyfriend even though she is too tired. She just doesn't want to disappoint anyone.

. . .

One physical attribute that Lerner does not discuss is overeating. I can relate to this one personally. Both K and S have weight issues. Both have dieted successfully, lost a lot of weight and then gained it back shortly after. T's stress is created through violence. He said he became very calm when stressed about potential violence (i.e., a potential fight). Recently the center staff were waiting for a pending conflict from a gang-related argument. T was calm around the teens but was very fidgety earlier in the day when only staff were present. R is currently taking medication to ward off panic attacks. She does not outwardly show her panic but she does take steps to avoid conflict and possible stress.

Janine remained an enigma to me until I found out about her disability. This explained her tenacity, her perfectionism, and her choice to remain separate from the humor that often emerged in the class. She was a serious student, far too serious as it continued to cause her to resist cooperation and collaboration. She wrote fluidly and when she added her personal experience, there was an increase in credibility and "bite." Janine's project involved interviews with people who had had recent experience with disabled services at local colleges: students, service providers, parents. Her summary included the following:

It became apparent that individuals are deeply affected by surplus powerlessness. The most common expression was the high degree of stress that resulted from their dealing with providers of the services, faculty, and other college administrators. Students faced the combined pressure of course work along with fight for services. Their reactions are anger, orneriness, isolation, frustration, failure, and powerlessness. The staff are stressed by school bureaucracy, vague guidelines in law, and lack of standard procedures. Isolation within school settings requires support from family and other groups outside school which is made difficult by the lack of trust and collaboration among students and parents with institutional staff.

Marilyn was an upper middle-class executive in the class and proved to be supervisor of the group that Gilda interviewed. Her study reported the effects of a computer company takeover, particularly on women who perceived themselves as competent and in control. It was intriguing how differently the male interviewee responded. She conducted her interviews in some amazing places: a hotel, car, lunch diner, and Chinese restaurant. Marilyn reported:

DVR is a small close-knit agency. There is a genuine concern for co-workers and we tend to know more about one another's personal lives and attitudes than is usual in the workplace. The intimate nature of the relationships developed with clients carries over to staff interactions. There is a sense of community that may be due in part to the nature of the work we do. However, the stress level has increased markedly in the past six months and the fall-out is becoming evident among the staff in general. Change is a constant in our lives, but when we perceive that we are powerless to impact it, direct, it or stop it, we experience fear. And fear is often expressed as anger. I am interested in determining the effects of change, increased stress levels, and compromised job security on staff who already give one hundred and fifty percent to jobs they view as high demand, low control. Five of the six (the male, the exception) are progressing through the early stages of grief.

Initially there was a sense of disbelief—this can't be happening to us, Congress can't mean us. Then came denial. "Even if they combine all employment services, we are different and we will survive." Now we are seeing anger and fear. "How could they do this to us." "This just isn't fair or right." The anger is being directed at authority. The fear is that the people higher up are not telling the truth or sharing what they know. Withholding information is a power issue. It would be interesting to correlate the anger at authority with what was learned as a child about power and authority. Lerner reminds us that anger is a catalyst for action. I will be interested to see if this group of people who are used to working autonomously, but who have developed a community of sorts at work, will be able to use their anger for positive change.

The content of these portraitures, the topics pursued in the research, as well as the complexity of the students' lives provide powerful insights into the iterative process of critical dialoging. The student researchers in the process of assessing their own lives, both professional and personal, reached out through interviews to individuals who offered perspectives that validated, enhanced, or corrected my students' views. Providing a safe space for reflection with appropriate probes and meaningful silences makes intervention possible.

CHAPTER 9

First Quarter Attrition: Community College Staff and Faculty Ask Why

URBAN COMMUNITY COLLEGE SITS LIKE A MODERN FACTORY ON A HILL amidst a very "hip" district near the city's Central District. The population is largely African American and Latino. Suburban Community College, in contrast, adjoins Interstate 5 across from a venerable shopping mall in a suburban neighborhood that is increasingly home to new and upwardly mobile Asian American families. Arrival at Lake Community College requires a sojourn to a wooded neighborhood that adjoins the fastest growing region in the state and home to many cutting-edge corporations. As different as they appear, these and nearly twenty other community colleges of the state serve as the first door of entry to higher education for many students, particularly, but certainly not exclusively, working-class students.

The attrition rate nationally for community college students is high; that it is most pronounced in the first quarter is alarming (Pascarella and Terenzini, 1991). Approximately one-third of community college students do not continue after the first quarter. The State Board of Technical and Community Colleges (SBTCC) wanted reasons and solutions. It contacted me to assist in helping it think through how research might be conducted on attrition that would provide it not only with data and a deeper understanding of what impedes progress into the second quarter but also with a research method that would stem the tide of loss and have a lasting impact on the institutions.

Physically, the work could not be done by one individual; the research had to be conducted early in the fall quarter across six campuses, some as far as three hundred miles apart. Realistically, as an outsider gathering data, I could collect vast amounts of information and gain significant insights but this would neither change the institutions nor the staff/faculty within them. I wanted statewide participation, and I wanted to use research that would have a transformative function. I decided that the most effective and efficient means to conduct research and transform the institutions was to train professionals within their own colleges to do the work. Although I knew some of the obstacles that students face and why they leave early, most of the staff who ended up participating in the research project claimed ignorance of these factors. Clearly, if I was going to get "buy-in" from these educators, I needed to find ways to engage them in conversations with their students; they themselves needed to hear about the numerous hurdles and bureaucratic hassles that alienate students who are already burdened by the multiple demands of work and family. If students' first encounters with higher education leave them frustrated and misunderstood, it is unlikely they will return. I needed to transform the way front-line staff, as well as faculty, saw their students and the challenge of first entry into higher education.

EARLY VALIDATION FOR FIRST-GENERATION ENTERING STUDENTS: RESEARCH ON FIRST-QUARTER RETENTION AT COMMUNITY COLLEGES

First impressions are significant, particularly if one encounters the unfamiliar. Movement from K–12 schooling or from the workforce into community colleges requires adjustment to new modes of operation. For some the transition comes with ease; for most it is confusing and frustrating. How students are received and treated within the first days and weeks of their first quarter may determine not only if they remain and persist but also how they view themselves and their education. First-generation college students with a tentative understanding of their role in higher education are particularly vulnerable (Tinto, 1987). What might be routine bureaucratic protocol for middle-class students can be misconstrued as a rejection, a rebuttal, or aloofness to students unfamiliar or uncomfortable with an institution of higher education. Questions of rightful place and adequacy can occlude the process.

To address these issues, I proposed an ethnographic, cross-state examination of how college programming designed to increase student persistence was working for first-generation college students early in their first quarter. Rendon's concept of validation (1989) provided by institutions of higher education for entering students is a positive, institutional focus for addressing the problem of early leaving. First-generation college students constitute an especially crucial population for understanding the role of community colleges in expanding higher education to new families and diverse cultural settings. There are a host of reasons why students do not persist in college, including family obligation, economic need, lack of academic preparation, and so on, most of which are summarized in the predictive concepts of "intent to leave" and "intent to stay." Such concepts appear to focus on the student but include the interplay of several institutional factors, most of which can be addressed by a college that intends to encourage its students to persist and to succeed. Ethnographic research is a form of intervention within the community. Rather than overlook the effect of the research, thoughtful intervention can be combined with illuminative findings. The result is not a set of data on early leaving or persistence that can be generalized to equivalent populations but a collection of insights that allow for more effective institutional attention to the needs of students.

Research about community college obstacles has drawn attention to "front-line" contacts with new students: recruitment, applications, admissions, parking, and security—services that students often encounter before they enter the student-faculty relationships and are the common focus of retention studies. Initial contacts with faculty can also be possible sources of early validation of students, for example, the process of seeking instructor permission to enter classes or the role of faculty in student orientation. Generally, students who are tentative about higher education are especially sensitive to the events of welcoming and hospitality, which provide validation in the earliest contacts with a college setting (Pace, 1979).

At the time of this project, all community colleges in the state had examined the problem of early leaving and put in place a wide array of services and programs designed to provide validation for entering students. Each college attempted to respond to its local communities from which most of the first-generation students came, including ethnic minorities, new immigrants, unemployed timber workers, veterans, and older women returning to work, etc. Attention to improved retention and success of students was a constant feature of institutional research at these institutions. Attempts to chart student persistence, rates of transfer, and other indicators of success emphasized the role of student-faculty interaction, course availability, student performance, and other academic factors. Qualitative studies using student and faculty interviews and narrative documents, morever, added to the emphasis on academic factors and supported the importance of curricular innovation, faculty development, adequate facilities and other features of a lively college program. A continuing concern, however, was the persistent attrition of new students during their first quarter of college. The demographic information on such "early leavers" did not clearly identify student characteristics associated with first-quarter attrition.

Training for the in-house researchers was completed during July and August in preparation for interviewing during the first month of the academic year. Interviews were to focus on first-generation, entering students from diverse ethnic, cultural, and occupational communities and to identify the elements of college programs and services that promote students' "intent to stay." The project also was designed to demonstrate a model of qualitative research that would offer positive intervention for students during their initial experience with a college. After discussion, we chose to focus on campus climate as an important factor in "early leaving." Given the nature of the issue, it seemed sensible to focus on the earliest phase of student experience on the college campus because that early experience provides the crucial foundation for further classroom and other academic experiences known to be important to continuing student success.

Students first gain knowledge of a community college and its hospitality in several ways: publicity, family members and friends, academic advising in high school or other advising services, campus visits, admissions procedures and testing, financial aid application, bookstore and other campus facilities, and, of course, classroom and other related activities. Campus experience, therefore, involves college staff, resources, facilities, services, and public information. Students who become "early leavers" are difficult to reach and may be gone before any formal contact is established; therefore, institutional research has generally neglected them unless they return and are later contacted as persisting students. A study of such early campus experience, therefore, had to reach out to students while they were actually having such experiences: offices and corridors, cafeterias, bookstores and other student services, and the first few class sessions.

In preparation for the training of the college researchers and the fall quarter interviewing process, I personally conducted site visits at three of the colleges, interviewing students from a range of socioeconomic, educational, and ethnic backgrounds. I interviewed six to twelve students at each campus using a protocol developed to explore each student's experience and perceptions of all aspects of the college encountered during the initial weeks of enrollment, including preenrollment contact. These site visits also served as an opportunity for me to identify and meet college personnel who could serve as in-house researchers.

I recruited a research team from each college and developed procedures as well as training for each team. I was to present the results to the faculty and staff of each campus for further comment and interpretation. The most important collaboration, intrinsic in the research process itself, however, included talking with students about their initial experiences and perceptions at each campus, seeking the suggestions of students for improvement, and, when appropriate, providing immediate intervention to meet student needs. During several workshops in the summer I began the process of training in ethnographic research methods. Sessions included interviewing practice using the project protocol, discussion of intervention concepts, methods for selection of interviewees, observation methods, and treatment of findings. The intent of the workshops was to give institutional researchers, accustomed to remaining inside the inner sanctums of administrative offices sorting through banks of numerical data, the skills and confidence to reach out and interact with the clientele that they claimed to understand and serve. The vast majority of these individuals had been trained to work in isolation with paper and machines; they were not pleased about moving out of their comfort zone. The idea that they would ultimately be responsible for conducting face to face conversations with first-quarter community college students proved devastating. Some could not handle it and did not complete the training. A few came to relish the opportunity to discover the real lives of their students. Several of the researchers were skeptical about the process at first. They presumed they knew why students dropped out.

The procedures for moving the in-house researchers along the continuum from fear to enthusiasm were rather straightforward. The workshops had to be well structured, allowing for small group and large group work. I could not allow for group dissent to stall the process. On the very first day as soon as the participants walked into the workshop, they received an agenda and directions to interview three people in the group whom they did not know. The lead question—what would someone not know about you by just looking at you?—instantly personalized the situation. After about ten minutes speaking to one person they were to go to another person and interview him or her, then to a third. The purpose was not for them to get to know each other, but rather to gain an essential skill in qualitative research: how to initiate a conversation with a stranger. While I admitted that the process was intrusive, I pointed out that its purpose was to help them get over their shyness. From this initial engagement I asked for volunteers to report back to the group about any interesting and unexpected information that they found. The purpose was two-fold: (1) to move them beyond visual expectations and bias, and (2) to see if they could accurately relay what they heard. Misrepresentation of an informant because of one's own filtering can contaminate the data. They needed to learn how to listen cleanly and openly.

I then wanted them to try asking an actual research question that could be used in interviewing. Like all interview questions, however, it had to be contextualized; it had to relate to the individual involved; it had to touch something in the interviewee that would make him or her want to talk about it, honestly and openly. It had to be meaningful. I asked these researchers about what in their profession gave them satisfaction. But before they could leap into another interviewing session, I had them break down the question into component parts and develop probes, varying the question in ways that would make it accessible to a range of people and contexts. We also discussed co-counseling skills, the importance of active listening, listening to one person fully before interjecting one's own views and life story, and how socioeconomic class, culture, educational background, linguistic codes, and immigrant status influence conversation patterning.

After the one-on-one interviews about career satisfaction, they began the coding and analysis of the responses. They then noted which parts of the interview were relevant to the question and which parts, while interesting, were not. From this one interview they saw how much could be gathered in a short period of time. The next step involved identifying themes. What reoccurred in terms of career satisfaction? What might cause variation? I explained to the trainees:

> You have to adapt what I have told you to your own style. It is important that you understand how the research process flows through you, including how you approach a student, how you introduce yourself, how you establish trust, how you explain the project, how you respond to the student with probes and follow ups. High-quality interviewing requires an attitude. Anyone can come up with a list of questions to ask a stranger; few people can effectively gather authentic information in a nonexploitative, nonhierarchical way in which you are serving the needs of the informant as much as satisfying the needs of the research. Protocol also includes the basics: what do you ask, what do you listen for, what do you take notes on? Clothes are important: no heels, suits, ties; dress to be able to sit on the floor. Carry all your stuff discreetly, in a handbag, backpack, or briefcase. Do not identify yourself based on

your institutional role. You are doing research for a statewide community college project. Gather data first, then you can offer assistance. Note how you, the researcher, is affected by the information given. Track your vulnerability and how you respond to things you may not have expected. Transcribe your tapes and write up your summary as soon as possible after the interview. Do not filter material when you summarize.

Some important issues arose during the development and training phases of the project. In order to fulfill the expectations set out for this particular research project, the college researchers needed to be familiar with campus programs and services as well as be willing to provide immediate intervention when student issues were identified during the interviews. They had to be committed to both the accurate assessment of student experiences and the improvement of the campus climate for students. Since critical ethnography and other qualitative research methods were not familiar to most of the college staff, careful training and modeling was necessary early in the development of the project. Support for the project from college administration was crucial at every stage of the research process. While the pilot work I had done at the three colleges was helpful to me to develop effective procedures, I did not share the findings from these interviews at the beginning for fear of creating premature expectations and generalizations.

RESULTS

I had the students prepare the results of the project in several phases and formats. They tape-recorded and transcribed as well as recorded the interviews by hand. They gathered and organized demographic information about the students interviewed at each campus. A training session that followed the completion of interviews included sharing preliminary findings among all campus teams. They prepared various forms of result summaries from each campus and shared them in writing and in presentations during college and statewide meetings. They forwarded interview materials and summaries to me.

One of the most profound results of the project was the impact that the knowledge gained from the interviews had on the college faculty and staff who served as interviewers. At a training session that occurred just after the completion of most of the interviews, each campus team was asked to consider:

- What common themes emerged from the interviews?
- How have you shared the results of the project so far?
- Have you done any follow-up interviews?
- How have you perceived the institution differently since the interviews?
- How have students viewed or accessed you differently?
- What do you do with the results hereafter? On your campus and for other audiences?
- How can a statewide focus on student transition to college be developed?

After extensive discussions, it became clear that the main concern of students was to access their classes and transfer to a four-year college or university. The researchers found that the vast majority of students obtain their orientation to, and information about, the college primarily from peers and/or previous students. The respondents up to that point had had little or no contact with administrators, faculty, or staff; they had not seen Student Services as an avenue for assistance or guidance.

STUDENT ISSUES

While the student interviews reflected many successful aspects of each campus, a sampling of problems concerning the student transition to college on at least some campuses included:

- Many students need help in overcoming the isolation of the college campus environment relative to their experience in high school.

- Many students view their initial experience on campus as a struggle through a morass without direction or adequate signage.
- Services perceived by the college as available and oriented to student needs are not adequately visible or understood by students.
- A number of students seemed to find a niche, both academically and socially, and then get stuck in it, fearing to venture into classes or encounter people who might require a stretch in their comfort level.
- Students need relevant reasons to connect to each other, particularly concerning academic interests.
- Classes (instructors) need to create opportunities for small group and interpersonal connections, discussions, and support groups.

EFFECTS ON THE INSTITUTIONS AND RESEARCHERS

The research was designed to create transformation on numerous levels. The concerns of students were to be made known to the faculty and staff who in turn would inform the administration. The research also involved immediate intervention. In the process of gathering data, the researchers were to offer suggestions, referrals, and other information to students as needed. The process of intervention linked students with people who could provide for their needs. It provided them with someone to discuss their concerns, a form of counseling that served a retention device in and of itself. For the faculty and staff interviewers, the process helped them make sense out of the complexity of student frustration. The process was symbiotic—in the act of gathering information, the encounter with students served as a helpful and necessary intervention.

As a result of the research, most of the faculty interviewers said that they had come to see their students in a new light, that they would never be able to teach with the same assumptions again. They realized that students have outside lives that need to be respected and taken into account, since they impact their academic expectations and performance. There was also an increased appreciation for different teaching methods in student learning and retention. One instructor said, "We are now kinder and gentler than before [prior to doing the research]. We know that our students live complex lives." Another stated, "I didn't have a clue about my students' lives. I just assumed that they showed up. I have a new-found respect for the community college." A third faculty member joined in, "I have been here for twenty years and always had a sense that students had a range of needs but I didn't know what they were. I have a better sense now."

College administrators and staff members came to understand, in a different way, the multiplicity of students' concerns and admitted that most of them had taken little opportunity to talk with or listen to their students prior to this work. They had a greater appreciation for the importance of things being handled "right" in the Student Services area. In response to the extensive interviewing and coding of data, one Student Services staff person said, "We didn't know what they needed until we asked!" In commenting on the lack of formal recognition or reward from the institution for talking to students, one faculty member stated, "If we aren't functioning as whole persons, or the institutional cultures don't treat us that way, how can we interact with students that way, or expect them to see the institution in those terms?"

The project also offered some side benefits for professional development. For example, collaboration and discussion of critical issues among staff and faculty members within and among colleges produced greater respect for, and knowledge of, each other's work. In one instance, a faculty member shared with one of the staff people in her group her knowledge of a sexual harassment case that had been confided to her by one of her interviewees. The faculty member remarked that had she not met some of the staff people during these research training sessions who specialized in such issues, she probably would not have spoken with anyone about the incident and remained impotent in providing options for this student and others like her in the future. Since the situation required the involvement of the international student advisor as well, the case was more complex, requiring several different levels of interventions. The teacher now knew which resources were available.

As an example of critical ethnography as action research, the interviewing process allowed students an opportunity to make sense out of complex issues that led to their frustration and early leave taking. An interested representative of the college greeted the inerviewees. As staff members listened to student concerns, they were able to respond to the students' personal and academic needs within the institution. In terms of institutional research, the project informed and complemented other efforts under way to study student attrition, leading to more effective research strategies. Through participation as researchers, college staff faced their own attitudes and questions about students and student experience, thus impacting their own career interests and work.

AFTERWORD

I HAVE ATTEMPTED TO ILLUSTRATE HOW CRITICAL DIALOGUE AS PEDAGOGY creates opportunities for increased awareness of our multiple identities as we simultaneously interrogate our assumptions of the Other. In all of the cases presented, ethnography served as an intervention in opening up dialogue so desperately needed to move beyond misconceptions and misinformation of the Other. I have presented a narrative of my attempts to create critical dialogues with students and for students with their students, families, and communities. The process has been largely one of discovery—discovery of self and of pedagogy. As I have moved to conceptualize my approach, the influence and precedents of the long traditions of dialogue and of critical theory have become more clear and have set me on yet further study. The work of Burbules (1993) and Sidorkin (1999) has been especially helpful in showing how Freire and other advocates of dialogic and critical pedagogy can be understood in light of Bakhtin and Buber as well as feminist and Marxist theory. Michrina and Richards (1996) offer a closely related and challenging approach to ethnographic fieldwork.

The implications of what I have shared in this book can best be seen in a set of guidelines that I strive to apply appropriately in each of the varied settings in which I have worked.

TRUST

A dialogue of trust between teacher and student begins with mutual disclosure of personal experience that is relevant to the issues of the course and/or the research project. Systematically, this occurs in two major ways.

Self portrait. I ask students to complete self-portraits that provide me with information about who is in my class and from whence they come. It alerts students to the reality that who they are is significant to how they will interpret and view the "texts" offered in the class. Although the self portrait asks for responses to specific questions, it allows students to expand selectively on issues about which they feel I should be aware. It also signals that the personal will be discussed in this class. For many this is a time for reflection and reassessment.

My story. The assumptions that students have about professors are amusing to say the least, but often damaging as we continue to allow young people to think that the road to academia is straight and narrow. By sharing my life story with its many twists and struggles, I become more real and more accessible to the students. They begin to see possibilities and opportunities whereas before there was only frustration. I become a bridge between their past, as it is often similar to my own, and their future. My openness with them, while surprising at first, inevitably brings them to share their life story with me either through writing or personal discussions.

ENGAGING RESEARCH

A research process that reconnects students with their home communities and identities allows for emotional engagement with the means and ends of research (Rist, 1983). To be transformative, research must be relevant to the pressing demands of young people's lives. There are few topics in education, sociology, anthropology, political science, or other academic disciplines that cannot be configured to engage the interests and lives of youth. Providing them with the opportunity to define research areas and develop research questions that can most accurately access the information desired not only honors their knowledge base but also allows for significant reflection and growth. Reconnection in the research process is more than a convenient motivator. Academic life rests on a norm of separation: of student from self, of student from family and community, of one student from another. The discovery of dialogue across all of those separations moves the student from passive to active participant, from witness to author.

DIFFICULT DIALOGUES

Dialogue among students based on critical readings that provide a larger context for the research process develops an informed understanding of personal issues and experience. The relevant readings are endless in their variety and work best when the instructor is also risking encounter with varied and challenging viewpoints and methods of inquiry. There is no substitute for demanding that students take risks academically. Few students like to stand before their peers to present controversial material, particularly when they know that this will be followed by questions from the audience. No matter how much resistance I have received from students when this idea is first brought up, students have always been pleased with themselves after having engaged in the process. More often than not they consider the experience a turning point in their education. As future leaders, whether it be in education or society at large, youth must learn to organize material for group observation, take a stand on critical issues, and defend their views in front of strangers.

I never ask for regurgitation of material but rather encourage the students to develop formats such as poster sessions, skits, debates, characterizations, mock-ups of school board or union meetings, musicals, poetry, and so forth. They can also remain within more traditional modes if that is more comfortable for them; regardless, all are assessed on the basis of their ability to project voice and on their presence. Group negotiation and respect that results from these events lasts far beyond the end of the quarter. Public presentation is best prepared in small-group informal settings and these are built into my pedagogy from the first class meetings to the last minute preparation for formal group presentations.

CONTINUOUS ASSESSMENT

Continual evaluation of the research process enlivens the course topics as well as developing crucial research skills. For instance, one's reaction to what occurs in a classroom might have more to do with one's predisposition than the situation itself. Providing opportunities and safe spaces for students to debrief from field experiences is essential. This process includes impromptu field notes, reflective essays on how the experience affected the interviewer, verbal disclosure, and structured research analysis. Field notes are no less valid than the polished essays. In my classes, students turn in everything.

INTERVENTION

By using ethnographic research, student educators can gain from the engagement with students and communities. My version of significant critical ethnography is that which intervenes in normal life and transforms both the interviewee and the interviewer. I teach my students how to remain respectful and observant without being detached. They learn how to ask questions that probe the obvious contradictions, whether they be in the community, in schools, or the family. I encourage them to offer information and intervene if it clarifies a misconception or eradicates a perceived wrong, and I remind them that they are in a privileged position. Intuition, sensitivity, and respect for all people are of utmost concern and essential for dialogue.

Finally, no matter how we crave clear demarcation lines between the infirm and the healthy, the incarcerated and the free, the rich and the poor, the young and the aged, we are all part of one continuum. Fear motivates us to maintain distance. Our comfort comes in separation from the reminders of that which we know is possible, if not inevitable, in our own lives. In my approach to both teaching and research, I seek to create a shift in the "political" landscape of higher education, especially teacher preparation. As future and veteran educators ask about and listen to the experience of those they seek to serve, they can reengage their own vocation. I hope my account of one coherent approach to pedagogy can help to create that reengagement.

References

Anyon, J. (1995). Race and social class and educational reform in an inner-city school. *Teachers College Record, 97*(1), 69–94.

Apple, M. W. (1982). *Education and power*. Boston: Routledge & Kegan Paul.

Aronowitz, S., & Giroux, H. A. (1991). *Postmodern education: Politics, culture, and social criticism*. Minneapolis: University of Minnesota.

Astin, A. W. (1993). *What matters in college: Four critical years revisited*. San Francisco: Jossey-Bass.

Ayers, W., & Ford, F. (Eds.). (1996). *City kids, City teachers*. New York: The New Press.

Becker, H. S. (1998). *Tricks of the trade: How to think about your research while you're doing it*. Chicago: University of Chicago Press.

Bhatti, G. (1999). *Asian children at home and at school*. London: Routledge.

Burbules, N. C. (1993). *Dialogue in teaching: Theory and practice*. New York: Teachers College Press.

Burleson, D. L. (Ed.). (1991). *Reflections: Personal essays by 33 distinguished educators*. Bloomington, IN: Phi Delta Kappa.

Bruner, J. (1990). *Acts of meaning*. Cambridge, MA: Harvard University Press.

Carspecken, P. F. (1996). *Critical ethnography in educational research*. New York & London: Routledge.

Chevigny, B. G. (1996). Mississippi learning: Algebra as political curriculum. *The Nation, 262*(9), 16–21.

Connell, R. W. (1989). Cool guys, swots and wimps: The interplay of masculinity and education. *Oxford Review of Education, 15*, 291–303.

Cummins, J. (1986). Empowering minority students: A framework for intervention. *Harvard Educational Review, 56*(1), 18–36.

Deever, B. (1990). Critical pedagogy: The concretization of possibility. *Contemporary Education, 61*(2), 71–76.

Duster, T. (1991). *The diversity project: Final report.* Berkeley, CA: University of California.

Epstein, J. L. (1986). Parents' reactions to teacher practices of parent involvement. *The elementary school, 86*(3), 277–294.

Erikson, F. (1987). Transformation and school success: The politics and culture of educational achievement. *Anthropology and Education Quarterly, 18*(4), 335–356.

Fairclough, N. (1989). *Language and power.* London: Longman.

Fine, M. (1991). *Framing dropouts: Notes on the politics of an urban high school.* Albany: State University of New York Press.

Fordham, S. (1996). *Blacked out: Dilemmas of race, identity, and success at Capital high.* Chicago: University of Chicago.

Foucault, M. (1988). *The care of the self: The history of sexuality,* (Vol. 3.). New York: Random House.

Freire, P. (1970). *Pedagogy of the oppressed.* New York: Continuum.

Freire, P., & Macedo, D. P. (1995). A dialogue: Culture, language, and race. *Harvard Educational Review, 65*(3), 377–402.

Fullilove, R. E. & Treisman, P. U. (1990). Mathematics achievement among African American undergraduates at the University of California, Berkeley: An evaluation of the mathematics workshop program. *Journal of Negro Education 59*(3), 463–478.

Gandara, P. (1995). *Over the ivy walls: The educational mobility of low-income Chicanos.* Berkeley, CA: California Policy Seminar.

Geertz, C. (1973). *The interpretation of cultures.* New York: Basic Books.

Gibson, M. A., & Ogbu, J. U. U. (Eds.). (1991). *Minority status and schooling: A comparative study of immigrant and involuntary minorities.* New York: Garland.

Gillborn, D. (1990). *'Race', ethnicity and education.* London: Unwin Hyman.

Glenn, C. L., & De Jong, E. J. (1996). *Educating immigrant children: Schools and language minorities in twelve nations.* New York: Garland.

Goodson, I. F., & Walker, R. (1991). *Biography, identity, and schooling: Episodes in educational research.* London: Falmer Press.

Gordon, J. A. (1994). Why students of color are not entering the field of teaching. *Journal of Teacher Education, 45*(5), 346–353.

Gordon, J. A. (1997a). A critical interpretation of policies for minority culture college students. *NACADA Journal, 17*(1), 15–21.

Gordon, J. A. (1997b). Teachers of color speak to issues of respect and image. *The Urban Review, 29*(1), 41–66.

Gordon, J. A. (2000a). *The color of teaching.* London: Routledge-Falmer Press.

Gordon, J. A. (2000b). Asian American resistance to selecting teaching as a career: The power of community and tradition. *Teachers College Record, 102*(1), 173–196 .

Gordon, J. A. (2000c) It's a fine line . . . Deconstructing youth at-risk: Critical ethnography as pedagogy. *Action in Teacher Education, 22*(2), 13–24.

Gougeon, T. D. (1993). Urban schools and immigrant families: Teacher perspectives. *The Urban Review, 25*(4), 251–287.

Greene, M. (1986). In search of a critical pedagogy. *Harvard Educational Review, 56,* 427–441.

Haberman, M. (1996). Selecting and preparing culturally competent teachers for urban schools. In J. Sikula (Ed.), *Handbook of research in teacher education.* 2d. (pp. 747–760). New York: Macmillan.

Hidalgo, N. M., McDowell, C. L., & Siddle, E. V. (Eds.). (1993). *Facing racism in education.* Cambridge, MA: Harvard Educational Review.

Holland, D. C., & Eisenhart, M. A. (1993). Women's ways of going to school: Cultural reproduction of women's identities as workers. In L. Weis & M. Fine (Eds.), *Beyond silenced voices: Class, race, and gender in United States schools* (pp. 266–301). New York: State University of New York Press.

Horton, M., and Freire, P. (1990). *We make road by walking: Conversations on education and social change.* Philadelphia: Temple University Press.

Hummel, M., and Steele, C. (1996). The learning community: A program to address issues of academic achievement and retention. *Journal of Intergroup Relations, 23*(2), 28–32.

Igoa, C. (1995). *The inner world of the immigrant child.* New York: St. Martin's Press.

Illich, I. (1970). *Deschooling society.* New York: Harper & Row.

Jehl, J., & Kirst, M. W. (1992). Getting ready to provide school linked services: What schools must do. *The future of children, 2*(1), 95–106.

Kozol, J. (1991). *Savage inequalities*. New York: Crown.

Laing, R. D. (1969). *The politics of the family and other essays*. New York: Vintage.

Lerner, M. (1992). *Surplus powerlessness: The psychodynamics of everyday life and the psychology of individual and social transformation*. Oakland, CA: Institute for Labor & Mental Health.

Levinson, B. A., & Holland, D. (1996). The cultural production of the educated person: An introduction. In B. A. Levinson, D. E. Foley, & D. C. Holland (Eds.), *The cultural production of the educated person: Critical ethnographies of schooling and local practice* (pp. 1–53). Albany, NY: State University of New York Press.

MacLeod, J. (1987). *Ain't no making it: Leveled aspirations in a low-income neighborhood*. Boulder, CO: Westview.

McCaleb, S. P. (1995). *Building communities of learners: A collaboration among teachers, students, families, and community*. Mahwah, NJ: Lawrence Erlbaum Associates.

McDermott, R. (1976). *Kids make sense: An ethnographic account of the interactional management of success and failure in one first grade classroom*. Unpublished doctoral dissertation, Stanford University, Stanford, CA.

McLaren, P. L. (1986). *Schooling as a ritual performance*. Boston: Routledge & Kegan Paul.

McLaren, P. L. (1989). *Life in schools: An introduction to critical pedagogy in the foundations of education*. New York: Longman.

Maracle, L. (1988). Education. In L. Maracle (Ed.), *I am woman*. North Vancouver, B.C.: Press Publisher Ltd.

Massey, D., & Denton, N. (1993). *American apartheid*. Cambridge, MA: Harvard University Press.

Michrina, B. P., & Richards, C. (1996). *Person to person: Fieldwork dialogue and the hermeneutic method*. Albany, NY: State University of New York Press.

Mishler, E. G. (1986). *Research interviewing: Context and narrative*. Cambridge, MA: Harvard University Press.

Moll, L. (1990). Social and instructional issues in educating "disadvantaged" students. In M. S. Knapp & P. M. Shields (Eds.), *Bet-*

ter schooling for the children of poverty: Alternatives to conventional wisdom. 2d. Washington, D.C.: U.S. Government Printing Office.

Montero-Sieburth, M. (1989). Restructuring teachers' knowledge for urban settings. *Journal of Negro Education, 58*(3) 332–344.

Oakley, A. (1981). Interviewing women: A contradiction in terms. In H. Roberts (Ed.), *Doing feminist research* . Boston: Routledge & Kegan Paul.

Ogbu, J. U. U. (1990). Minority education in comparative perspective. *Journal of Negro Education, 59*(1), 45–56.

Ogbu, J. U. U. (1991). Immigrant and involuntary minorities in comparative perspective. In M. A. Gibson & J. U. U. Ogbu (Eds.), *Minority status and schooling: A comparative study of immigrant and involuntary minorities* (pp. 3–33). New York: Garland Publishing.

Ogbu, J. U. U. (1995). Cultural problems in minority education: Their interpretations and consequences—Part one: Theoretical background. *The Urban Review, 27*(3), 189–205.

Ogbu, J. U. U., and Simons, H. D. (1998). Voluntary and involuntary minorities: A cultural-ecological theory of school performance with some implications for education. *Anthropology and Education Quarterly, 29*(2), 155–188.

O'Loughlin, M., & Campbell, M. B. (1988). Teacher preparation, teacher empowerment, and reflective inquiry: A critical perspective. *Teacher Education Quarterly,15*(4), 25–53.

Pace, C. R. (1979). *Measuring outcomes of college: Fifty years of findings and recommendations for the future.* San Francisco: Jossey-Bass.

Pascarella, E. T., & Terenzini, P. T. (1991). *How college affects students: Findings and insights from twenty years of research.* San Francisco: Jossey-Bass.

Perry, T., & Fraser, J. (1993). *Freedom's plow.* New York: Routledge.

Phelan. P., Davidson, A. L., & Yu, H. C. (1998). *Adolescents' worlds: Negotiating family, peers, and school.* New York: Teachers College Press.

Rendon, L. I. (1989). The lie and the hope: Making higher education a reality for at-risk students. *American Association of Higher Education Bulletin*, May, 4–7.

Rist, R. C. (1983). Transmitting the craft. *Anthropology and Education Quarterly, 14*(3), 202–205.

Rist, R. C. (1994). Influencing the policy process with qualitative research. In Y. S. Lincoln & N. K. Denzin (Eds.), *Handbook of qualitative research* (pp. 545–558). Thousand Oaks, CA: Sage Publications.

Rosaldo, R. (1989). *Culture and truth: The remaking of social analysis*. Boston: Beacon Press.

Rose, M. (1988). *Lives on the boundary: The struggles and achievement of America's underprepared*. New York: Free Press.

Rothenberg, P. S. (1992). *Race, class, and gender in the United States: An integrated study*. New York: St. Martin's Press.

Rumbaut, R. G. (1995). The new Californians: Comparative research findings on the educational progress of immigrant children. In R. G. Rumbaut & W. A. Cornelius (Eds.), *California's immigrant children* (chap. 2). San Diego, CA: University of California Press.

Rumbaut, R. G., & Cornelius, W. A. (Eds.). (1995). *California's immigrant children*. San Diego, CA: University of California Press.

Sarason, S. B. (1982). *The culture of the school and problems of change*. Boston, MA: Allyn & Bacon.

Shor, I. (1980). The working class goes to college. In I. Shor (Ed.), *Critical teaching in everyday life* (pp.1–44). Boston: South End Press.

Shorris, E. (1992). *Latinos: A biography of the people*. New York: Norton.

Sidorkin, A. M. (1999). *Beyond discourse: Education, the self, and dialogue*. Albany, NY: State University of New York Press.

Sklar, H. (1995). *Chaos or community*. Boston: South End Press.

Smith, G. (Ed.) (1993). *Change/education: Issues in perspective*. DeKalb, IL: LEPS Press, Northern Illinois University.

Solomon, P. R. (1992). *Black resistance in high school: Forging a separatist culture*. Albany: State University of New York Press.

Spindler, G. D., Spindler, L., Williams, M., & Trueba, H. T. (1990). *The American cultural dialogue and its transmission*. Bristol, PA: Falmer Press.

Stanfield, J. H. I. (1994). Ethnic modeling in qualitative research. In N. R. Denzin, and Y. S. Lincoln (Eds.), *Handbook of qualita-*

tive research (pp. 175–188). Thousand Oaks: Sage Publications.

Steele, C. M. (1992). Race and the schooling of Black Americans. *Atlantic Monthly, 269*(4), 68–78.

Suarez-Orozco, M. M. (1991). Immigrant adaptation to schooling: A Hispanic case. In M. A. Gibson, & J. U. U. Ogbu (Eds.), *Minority status and schooling: A comparative study of immigrant and involuntary minorities*, (pp. 37–61). New York: Garland Publishing.

Takaki, R. (1989). *Strangers from a different shore: A history of Asian Americans*. Boston, MA: Little, Brown and Co.

Thomas, J. (1993). *Doing critical ethnography*. Newbury Park, CA: Sage Publications.

Tinto, V. (1987). *Leaving college: Rethinking the causes and cures of student attrition*. Chicago: University of Chicago Press.

Vasquez, O. A., Pease-Alvarez, L., & Shannon, S. M. (1994). *Pushing boundaries: Language and culture in a mexicano community*. New York: Cambridge University Press.

Velez-Ibanez, C. G., & Greenberg, J. B. (1992). Formation and Transformation of Funds of Knowledge Among U.S.-Mexican Households. *Anthropology and Education Quarterly, 23* (4), 313–335.

Vella, J. K. (1997). *Learning to listen: Learning to teach: The power of dialogue in educating adults*. San Francisco: Jossey-Bass.

Villegas, A. M. (1988). School failure and cultural mismatch: Another view. *The Urban Review, 20* (4), 253–265.

Weis, L. (1985). *Between two worlds: Black students in an urban community college*. New York: Routledge & Kegan Paul.

Woodring, P. (1983). *The persistent problem of education*. Bloomington, IN: Phi Delta Educational Foundation.

Zhou, M., & Bankston, C. L. (1998). *Growing up American: How Vietnamese children adapt to life in the United States*. New York: Russell Sage Foundation.

Index